The Strange Case of
Dr Jekyll and
Mr Hyde

Robert Louis Stevenson

OXFORD
UNIVERSITY PRESS

Contents

Introduction

What are Oxford Literature Companions?

Oxford Literature Companions is a series designed to provide you with comprehensive support for popular set texts. You can use the Companion alongside your novel, using relevant sections during your studies or using the book as a whole for revision.

Each Companion includes detailed guidance and practical activities on:

- **Plot and Structure**
- **Context**
- **Characters**
- **Language**
- **Themes**
- **Skills and Practice**

How does this book help with exam preparation?

As well as providing guidance on key areas of the novel, throughout this book you will also find 'Upgrade' features. These are tips to help with your exam preparation and performance.

In addition, in the extensive **Skills and Practice** chapter, the **Exam skills** section provides detailed guidance on areas such as how to prepare for the exam, understanding the question, planning your response and hints for what to do (or not do) in the exam.

In the **Skills and Practice** chapter there is also a bank of **Sample questions** and **Sample answers**. The **Sample answers** are marked and include annotations and a summative comment.

How does this book help with terminology?

Throughout the book, key terms are **highlighted** in the text and explained on the same page. There is also a detailed **Glossary** at the end of the book that explains, in the context of the novel, all the relevant literary terms highlighted in this book.

How does this book work?

Each book in the Oxford Literature Companions series follows the same approach and includes the following features:

- **Key quotations** from the novel
- **Key terms** explained on the page and linked to a complete glossary at the end of the book
- **Activity boxes** to help improve your understanding of the novel
- **UpGrade** tips to help prepare you for your exam

To help illustrate the features in this book, here are two annotated pages taken from this Oxford Literature Companion:

Key terms explained on the page and at the end of the book

Activity boxes to help improve your understanding of the novel

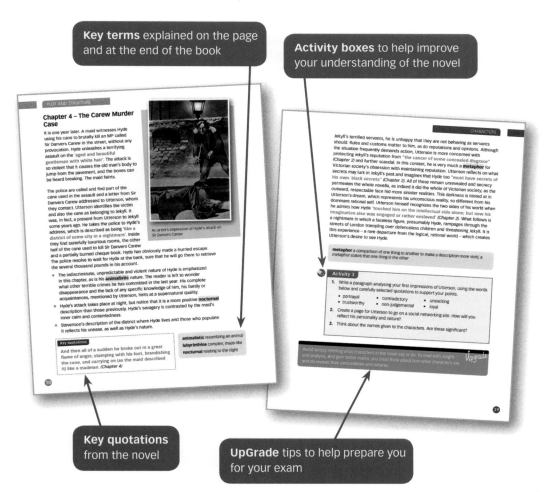

PLOT AND STRUCTURE

Chapter 4 – The Carew Murder Case

It is one year later. A maid witnesses Hyde using his cane to brutally kill an MP called Sir Danvers Carew in the street, without any provocation. Hyde unleashes a terrifying assault on the 'aged and beautiful gentleman with white hair'. The attack is so violent that it causes the old man's body to jump from the pavement, and the bones can be heard breaking. The maid faints.

The police are called and find part of the cane used in the assault and a letter from Sir Danvers Carew addressed to Utterson, whom they contact. Utterson identifies the victim and also the cane as belonging to Jekyll. It was, in fact, a present from Utterson to Jekyll some years ago. He takes the police to Hyde's address, which is described as being 'like a district of some city in a nightmare'. Inside they find tastefully luxurious rooms, the other half of the cane used to kill Sir Danvers Carew and a partially burned cheque book. Hyde has obviously made a hurried escape. The police resolve to wait for Hyde at the bank, sure that he will go there to retrieve the several thousand pounds in his account.

An artist's impression of Hyde's attack on Sir Danvers Carew

- The indiscriminate, unpredictable and violent nature of Hyde is emphasized in this chapter, as is his **animalistic** nature. The reader is left to wonder what other terrible crimes he has committed in the last year. His complete disappearance and the lack of any specific knowledge of him, his family or acquaintances, mentioned by Utterson, hints at a supernatural quality.
- Hyde's attack takes place at night, but notice that it is a more positive **nocturnal** description than those previously. Hyde's savagery is contrasted by the maid's inner calm and contentedness.
- Stevenson's description of the district where Hyde lives and those who populate it reflects his unease, as well as Hyde's nature.

Key quotations

And then all of a sudden he broke out in a great flame of anger, stamping with his foot, brandishing the cane, and carrying on (as the maid described it) like a madman. *(Chapter 4)*

animalistic resembling an animal
labyrinthine complex, maze-like
nocturnal relating to the night

10

CHARACTERS

Jekyll's terrified servants, he is unhappy that they are not behaving as servants should. Rules and customs matter to him, as do reputations and opinions. Although the situation frequently demands action, Utterson is more concerned with protecting Jekyll's reputation from "the cancer of some concealed disgrace" *(Chapter 2)* and further scandal. In this context, he is very much a **metaphor** for Victorian society's obsession with maintaining reputation. Utterson reflects on what secrets may lurk in Jekyll's past and imagines that Hyde "must have secrets of his own: black secrets" *(Chapter 2)*. All of these remain unrevealed and secrecy permeates the whole novella, as indeed it did the whole of Victorian society, as the outward, respectable face hid more sinister realities. This darkness is hinted at in Utterson's dream, which represents his unconscious reality, so different from his dominant rational self. Utterson himself recognizes the two sides of his world when he admits how Hyde 'touched him on the intellectual side alone; but now his imagination also was engaged or rather enslaved' *(Chapter 2)*. What follows is a nightmare in which a faceless figure, presumably Hyde, rampages through the streets of London trampling over defenceless children and threatening Jekyll. It is this experience – a rare departure from the logical, rational world – which creates Utterson's desire to see Hyde.

metaphor a comparison of one thing to another to make a description more vivid; a metaphor states that one thing is the other

Activity 3

1. Write a paragraph analysing your first impressions of Utterson, using the words below and carefully selected quotations to support your points.
   - portrayal
   - trustworthy
   - contradictory
   - non-judgemental
   - unexciting
   - loyal
2. Create a page for Utterson to go on a social networking site. How will you reflect his personality and nature?
3. Think about the names given to the characters. Are these significant?

Avoid simply retelling what characters in the novel say or do. To read with insight and analysis, and gain better marks, you must think about *how* what characters say and do reveals their personalities and natures.

Upgrade

39

Key quotations from the novel

UpGrade tips to help prepare you for your exam

Plot

Chapter 1 – Story of the Door

Mr Gabriel Utterson, a lawyer, is walking through a smart part of London with his distant cousin, Mr Richard Enfield. Their attention is caught by a dilapidated building and its rundown front door. The sight of it causes Enfield to remember an event he witnessed while returning home at about 3 a.m. one winter morning; he recalls how he saw a man accidentally knock down a young girl and then casually trample over her body, leaving her in distress.

Outraged, Enfield tells how he chased and caught the man, returning him to the scene of the crime where a tense stand-off developed with the girl's family. He says that everyone present was filled with an intense hatred of the man, who showed a strange mixture of both detachment and fear. Under threat, the man agreed to pay the family one hundred pounds in compensation. He took Enfield, a doctor and the girl's father back to this same door, returning from inside with some money and a cheque for the remainder. The cheque, surprisingly, was signed with the name of another, well-respected person. The man was held captive at Enfield's house until the morning so that they could go to the bank, where much to Enfield's surprise, the cheque was cashed without question.

Enfield reveals that the culprit was called Mr Hyde and explains how there was **"something downright detestable"** in his appearance. Utterson reveals that he too knows the identity of the man who signed the cheque. Both men suspect blackmail. Not wanting to gossip, they agree never to discuss the matter again.

"THE FELLOW HAD A KEY"

Hyde enters the neglected door in an illustration drawn by Edmund J Sullivan for the 1928 publication of the novella

- Mr Gabriel Utterson, a key character, is introduced. He is portrayed as something of a contradiction, a man who is **'cold… yet somehow lovable'**, introducing the theme of **duality**.

- The setting of London is established and the theme of duality is further reflected in the rundown door surrounded by neatly presented, colourful shop fronts.

- Enfield describes Hyde's brutal actions and lack of conscience. He emphasizes the intensity of feeling Hyde provokes in others. Hyde's connection to Jekyll is established.

- Utterson is a key **narrator**, although the **novella** has **multiple perspectives**. He participates in the action and, consequently, his limited knowledge is what he shares with the reader.

> **Key quotations**
>
> "... there was the man in the middle, with a kind of black, sneering coolness—frightened too, I could see that—but carrying it off, sir, really like Satan." *(Chapter 1)*
>
> "I never saw a man I so disliked, and yet I scarce know why." *(Chapter 1)*

duality the quality of being two things or split into two parts; the idea that we have two sides to our natures

multiple perspective narrative a story told from the point of view of more than one narrator

narrator the person who tells a story

novella a prose text which is longer than a short story but shorter than a standard novel

> **Activity 1**
>
> 1. Look at the description of the building and the door. Identify and explore quotations suggesting the ideas of mystery and secrecy.
>
> 2. What is the effect on the reader of having a narrator whose knowledge of events is limited?

Chapter 2 – Search for Mr Hyde

Utterson reveals that he has Dr Henry Jekyll's will. Its instructions worry him. They state that if anything happens to Jekyll, everything he owns should go to Mr Edward Hyde. Utterson now believes that Hyde is blackmailing Jekyll in order to stay silent about past crimes.

Utterson visits Dr Hastie Lanyon, a mutual friend of his and Jekyll, for advice. Lanyon explains that he has not seen Jekyll for some time and has no knowledge of a Mr Hyde. It becomes clear that there is conflict between Lanyon and Jekyll due to the nature of Jekyll's scientific work, which Lanyon angrily dismisses as "balderdash".

That night, Utterson dreams of an unidentified figure trampling over a child and of Jekyll being menaced by a faceless figure. These images are so intense that he develops a deep curiosity to see Mr Hyde in person. He loiters by the rundown door waiting for Hyde, who eventually appears. When approached and greeted by Utterson, Hyde shows his face 'with an air of defiance'.

In conversation, Hyde reveals his home address. The impact of the encounter is immense on Utterson, who is filled with 'disgust, loathing and fear' for Hyde, but cannot explain why he feels as he does.

Utterson visits Dr Jekyll at his home. Poole, Jekyll's butler, reveals that the servants see little of their master, who has ordered them to do whatever Hyde demands. Utterson reflects on what terrible crime his friend must have done and admits Jekyll "was wild when he was young", confessing also to 'many ill things' he has done himself. His worry is that Hyde is a danger to Jekyll and may seek to gain the inheritance from the will sooner rather than later. Utterson decides to protect his friend from the evil parasite that he believes is blackmailing him.

- The content of Jekyll's will is revealed, making the reader curious about the true nature of the relationship between Jekyll and Hyde, and also what Jekyll may have done in the past that he wishes to keep secret.

- Dr Lanyon is introduced, leaving the reader to speculate about Jekyll's scientific work and why it caused the friends to argue.

- Hyde appears for the first time. The physical repulsion he causes in others is reinforced. Note also the inability to accurately describe or explain this disgust. Hyde's animal-like quality is suggested.

- The interconnectedness of Jekyll's house with the laboratory and what is now revealed as the "old dissecting room door" from Chapter 1 is emphasized.

- The reader now embarks with Utterson on a quest for answers.

Key quotations

Mr Hyde was pale and dwarfish, he gave an impression of deformity without any nameable malformation, he had a displeasing smile, he had borne himself to the lawyer with a sort of murderous mixture of timidity and boldness, and he spoke with a husky, whispering and somewhat broken voice; all these were points against him, but not all of these together could explain the hitherto unknown disgust, loathing and fear with which Mr Utterson regarded him. "There must be something else," said the perplexed gentleman. "There *is* something more, if I could find a name for it. God bless me, the man seems hardly human!" *(Chapter 2)*

Chapter 3 – Dr Jekyll was Quite at Ease

It is two weeks later. Jekyll throws a dinner party at his house and appears in good spirits. In private, Utterson raises the will, its directions and his concerns about Hyde's nature with Jekyll. At the mention of Hyde's name, Jekyll changes, refusing to discuss the matter. Utterson, however, is persistent and asks Jekyll to trust him, assuring him that he will help. Jekyll thanks Utterson for his concern and assures him that he does trust him, while criticizing Dr Lanyon as **"a hide-bound pedant"**. He reassures him that he has the situation in hand and then asks him not to discuss the matter any further.

The chapter ends with Jekyll asking Utterson to ensure that Hyde gets what is outlined in his will, saying, **"I do sincerely take a great, a very great interest in that young man"**. Utterson agrees to respect this request, despite his very serious reservations.

- Initially, Stevenson introduces Jekyll here in good health and happy mood so that his later decline has something to be compared against.
- The tension between Jekyll and Lanyon is further reinforced.
- Utterson agrees to something that he is very uneasy about doing – executing Jekyll's will in favour of Hyde.

> **Key quotations**
>
> "It can make no change. You do not understand my position," returned the doctor, with a certain incoherency of manner. "I am painfully situated, Utterson; my position is a very strange—a very strange one. It is one of those affairs that cannot be mended by talking." *(Chapter 3)*
>
> "… indeed it isn't what you fancy; it is not so bad as that; and just to put your good heart at rest, I will tell you one thing: the moment I choose, I can be rid of Mr Hyde." *(Chapter 3)*

 Activity 2

1. Utterson is like an amateur detective attempting to unravel a mystery. How do the chapters' titles suggest the idea of a detective at work?

2. Why does he agree to do something he feels so easy about in relation to the will?

3. Which phrases suggest the animal-like quality of Hyde in his encounter with Utterson? What physical contrasts are suggested between Hyde and Jekyll?

4. An air of secrecy dominates. Make a note of references to keeping secrets, staying quiet about certain things or locking things away from others in Chapters 1–3.

Knowing the plot of *The Strange Case of Dr Jekyll and Mr Hyde* is important for your exam, but avoid simply retelling the story in your answer as this will not secure you a high mark.

Chapter 4 – The Carew Murder Case

It is one year later. A maid witnesses Hyde using his cane to brutally kill an MP called Sir Danvers Carew in the street, without any provocation. Hyde unleashes a terrifying assault on the 'aged and beautiful gentleman with white hair'. The attack is so violent that it causes the old man's body to jump from the pavement, and the bones can be heard breaking. The maid faints.

The police are called and find part of the cane used in the assault and a letter from Sir Danvers Carew addressed to Utterson, whom they contact. Utterson identifies the victim and also the cane as belonging to Jekyll. It was, in fact, a present from Utterson to Jekyll some years ago. He takes the police to Hyde's address, which is described as being 'like a district of some city in a nightmare'. Inside they find tastefully luxurious rooms, the other half of the cane used to kill Sir Danvers Carew and a partially burned cheque book. Hyde has obviously made a hurried escape. The police resolve to wait for Hyde at the bank, sure that he will go there to retrieve the several thousand pounds in his account.

An artist's impression of Hyde's attack on Sir Danvers Carew

- The indiscriminate, unpredictable and violent nature of Hyde is emphasized in this chapter, as is his **animalistic** nature. The reader is left to wonder what other terrible crimes he has committed in the last year. His complete disappearance and the lack of any specific knowledge of him, his family or acquaintances, mentioned by Utterson, hints at a supernatural quality.

- Hyde's attack takes place at night, but notice that it is a more positive **nocturnal** description than those previously. Hyde's savagery is contrasted by the maid's inner calm and contentedness.

- Stevenson's description of the district where Hyde lives and those who populate it reflects his unease, as well as Hyde's nature.

Key quotations

And then all of a sudden he broke out in a great flame of anger, stamping with his foot, brandishing the cane, and carrying on (as the maid described it) like a madman. *(Chapter 4)*

---

animalistic resembling an animal
labyrinthine complex; maze-like
nocturnal relating to the night

Activity 3

1. How does Stevenson create sympathy for Sir Danvers Carew in his description of him and how does this impact on the reader's opinion of Hyde? Do you think it is significant that the victim is an MP?

2. Choose quotations that compare the descriptions of Hyde and Carew to complete the table below.

Sir Danvers Carew	Hyde
'a very pretty manner of politeness'	'seemed to listen with an ill-contained impatience'

3. How does Stevenson reinforce the key theme of duality through minor characters and setting in this chapter?

Chapter 5 – Incident of the Letter

Utterson visits Jekyll at his laboratory. He finds him there, very unwell. Jekyll tells Utterson that Hyde has fled London and begs him to believe this is true. As evidence, he produces a letter from Hyde, delivered that morning by hand according to Jekyll, which seems to confirm this. The letter also apologizes for abusing Jekyll's generosity. Jekyll states that he is finished with Hyde for good and now fears for his own reputation. He asks that Utterson take the letter and consider what should be done with it.

While Utterson is convinced that Hyde intended to murder Jekyll to gain the proceeds of the will, Jekyll merely acknowledges that he has **"had a lesson"**, appearing exhausted and regretful. Utterson's suspicions are aroused further when Poole contradicts Jekyll, assuring Utterson that no one delivered a letter by hand to the house that morning.

Utterson decides to have the handwriting in the letter compared with that of Jekyll's (from a dinner invitation) by his trusted head clerk, Mr Guest, an expert in handwriting. Mr Guest finds the two samples identical but differently sloped. Utterson is stunned, believing Jekyll to have forged the letter to protect the murderous Hyde.

- Jekyll's portrayal in this chapter differs greatly from the way he is portrayed at the start of Chapter 3.
- More is revealed about the **labyrinthine** nature of Jekyll's residence.
- It is Mr Guest who perceives the similarity in the handwriting of Jekyll and Hyde, not Utterson. Utterson is more concerned with ensuring that Jekyll's reputation is not ruined by scandal than reporting Jekyll, who he suspects has forged for a murderer.

Key quotations

The fire burned in the grate; a lamp was set lighted on the chimney shelf, for even in the houses the fog began to lie thickly; and there, close up to the warmth, sat Dr Jekyll, looking deadly sick. He did not rise to meet his visitor, but held out a cold hand and bade him welcome in a changed voice. *(Chapter 5)*

Activity 4

1. Complete the table below, comparing how Jekyll is portrayed at the beginning of Chapters 3 and 5, using evidence from the text to support your descriptions.

How Jekyll is described in Chapter 3	How Jekyll is described in Chapter 5
healthy ('large, well-made')	

2. Using the quotations from your completed table, write a paragraph comparing the portrayal of Jekyll, using the following connectives of contrast: *however, in contrast, on the other hand.*

3. Look at the descriptions in Chapters 1–5 of Hyde's residence and the block in which it is situated. Draw a sketch of his home and the neighbouring buildings, labelling the various parts.

4. How can Jekyll's residence be seen as reflective of the human mind?

5. Discuss the fact that it is Guest who notices the similarity in the handwriting of Hyde and Jekyll. How does this impact on Utterson's credibility?

Chapter 6 – Remarkable Incident of Dr Lanyon

Hyde is still missing. There is a huge public reaction to Sir Danvers Carew's murder and a reward is offered for Hyde's capture. Jekyll is transformed for two months, becoming much more sociable and carrying out acts of charity and kindness. He throws a dinner party, which is attended by Utterson and Lanyon. It is like old times. This stops abruptly, however, and he becomes reclusive once again, refusing to see anyone.

Utterson visits Lanyon and is appalled to find him a terrified, nervous wreck, who seems close to death. In this chapter, Lanyon claims to have **"had a shock [...] and I shall never recover"**. At the very mention of Jekyll's name, he becomes emotional and tells Utterson that he does not want to even hear the name. He explains that all will be revealed after he dies.

Utterson writes to Jekyll, telling him of Lanyon's situation. The reply worries Utterson as Jekyll states that he wants to be left alone to deal with his own terrible sufferings, which he acknowledges are of his own making.

Within three weeks, Lanyon dies. On the night of the funeral, Utterson opens a package from Lanyon, which contains instructions that he should not open the papers within it until Jekyll's death or disappearance. Utterson resists the urge to open and read the contents, despite being greatly tempted. He visits Jekyll but is 'relieved to be denied admittance'. Poole reveals that Jekyll is now spending the vast majority of his time in a room above his laboratory and is very rarely seen.

- Jekyll's return to good spirits and improved health, albeit short-lived, coincides with the disappearance of Hyde.

- Speculation about the nature of the relationship between Lanyon and Hyde, and what has gone on between them, deepens. Lanyon's death, which he himself predicted, causes further intrigue.

- Again, the characters refuse to talk and discuss matters openly. The truth is hidden in letters, packages and paperwork with strict instructions about who can read them and when. This delays the exposure of truth and creates tension.

Key quotations

He had his death-warrant written legibly upon his face. The rosy man had grown pale; his flesh had fallen away; he was visibly balder and older; and yet it was not so much these tokens of a swift physical decay that arrested the lawyer's notice, as a look in the eye and quality of manner that seemed to testify to some deep-seated terror of the mind. *(Chapter 6)*

"I mean from henceforth to lead a life of extreme seclusion; you must not be surprised, nor must you doubt my friendship, if my door is often shut even to you. You must suffer me to go my own dark way. I have brought on myself a punishment and a danger that I cannot name. If I am the chief of sinners, I am the chief of sufferers also." *(Chapter 6)*

Chapter 7 – Incident at the Window

The following Sunday, Utterson and Enfield go for a walk. They stop at Jekyll's residence and enter the courtyard, where they see Jekyll sitting at an upstairs window. He appears sad, but engages them in conversation. Suddenly, 'an expression of such abject terror and despair' overtakes him and he shuts the window. Utterson and Enfield are stunned and confused by what they have witnessed. They walk home in silence with Utterson able to offer nothing more than, "God forgive us, God forgive us".

- There is a deep **irony** in Enfield's statement at the start of the chapter that they will not see Hyde again.

- The silence between Utterson and Enfield at the end echoes that of many others who have been unable to articulate (express) their feelings on meeting Hyde. This leaves the reader to draw their own conclusions about what the two saw and the relationship between Jekyll and Hyde.

- Events here immediately follow Lanyon's refusal to talk about his revelation in the previous chapter. The reader is left to ask if these experiences are in some way connected.

> **Key quotations**
>
> "Well," said Enfield, "that story's at an end at least. We shall never see more of Mr Hyde." *(Chapter 7)*
>
> The middle one of the three windows was half way open; and sitting close beside it, taking the air with an infinite sadness of mien, like some disconsolate prisoner, Utterson saw Dr Jekyll. *(Chapter 7)*

irony the discrepancy between what a character could be expected to do and what they actually do, often for comic effect

Activity 5

1. Why do you think this chapter is so short? Is this deliberate on Stevenson's part?

2. Utterson and Enfield are left speechless by what they witness and unable to find language to accurately describe what they see on Jekyll's face. Why is this?

3. Make a list of all the times to date when a character has refused to speak about something, agreed not to talk further or there is a reference to remaining silent.

In your answer, make sure you point out to the examiner how the author has deliberately structured the novel in a specific way to achieve a certain effect or emphasize a specific point.

Chapter 8 – The Last Night

Utterson is visited at his home by an anxious Poole, who suspects that his master has been killed by Hyde. He asks Utterson to investigate and they go to Jekyll's house.

Poole leads a nervous Utterson to the small room (the cabinet) by Jekyll's laboratory and announces him. The voice that replies is not Jekyll's and Poole suspects he was murdered eight days ago, explaining that he heard Jekyll utter a terrible cry from within and he has not seen him since. Utterson remains sceptical.

Poole explains that communication with the being in the room has been via notes, which urgently and repeatedly request a particular drug. However, each time the drug is fetched, it has been rejected for its impurity. A copy of one of the notes, in Poole's possession, is signed by Jekyll.

Poole has also seen the person in the room, although briefly. It was wearing a mask, cried out like a rat when it saw him and ran away. Utterson believes that Jekyll is seized by an illness that can **"both torture and deform the sufferer"**, but the servant states that he believes that the creature is Hyde.

Utterson demands entry to the room, but the voice inside refuses and begs for mercy. Utterson breaks down the door with the help of Poole and the footman. They find Hyde dead but **'still twitching'**, dressed in oversized clothes and holding **'the crushed phial in the hand'**. It is suicide. They search everywhere for Jekyll, inside and out, but do not find him. Instead they find his will, which has been amended to make Utterson the beneficiary. A second document tells Utterson to read Lanyon's papers and Jekyll's confession. Utterson urges those present to keep events secret and leaves to read both documents.

- Poole is used to develop the plot at this point.
- **Personification** is used to emphasize the power of the wind, suggesting some supernatural force at work and creating a sinister atmosphere.
- Utterson remains completely at a loss as to what has happened. He offers rather wild explanations. Poole is much more accurate in his assessment of the identity of the figure in the room.
- Familiar points arise again: the animalistic description of Hyde, the horror he evokes and the labyrinthine nature of Jekyll's residence.
- Lanyon's and Jekyll's documents, now in Utterson's possession, are the device that will unravel the mystery.

personification a type of metaphor where human qualities are given to objects or ideas

Key quotations

"All this last week (you must know) him, or it, or whatever it is that lives in that cabinet, has been crying night and day for some sort of medicine and cannot get it to his mind… This drug is wanted bitter bad, sir, whatever for." *(Chapter 8)*

"Well, when that masked thing like a monkey jumped from among the chemicals and whipped into the cabinet, it went down my spine like ice. O, I know it's not evidence, Mr Utterson; I'm book-learned enough for that; but a man has his feelings, and I give you my bible-word it was Mr Hyde!" *(Chapter 8)*

Chapter 9 – Dr Lanyon's Narrative

Utterson reads the document written by Lanyon. It tells of a strange request by Jekyll who asked that Lanyon remove a particular drawer from a room in Jekyll's house and bring it back to his own. A messenger, he was informed, would collect it from him at midnight.

Lanyon writes that out of curiosity and due to the somewhat desperate tone of the demand, he agreed but armed himself with a revolver. It took a carpenter and locksmith to unlock the cupboard containing the drawer, but they did so and Utterson removed it.

The messenger duly arrived at midnight to collect the contents and Lanyon was struck by the ridiculous appearance of the man. It was clearly Hyde. He was agitated and nearly hysterical at the sight of the contents of the drawer, which he used to mix a potion. This changed from red to dark purple and finally to a light green. Hyde offered Lanyon the choice of watching what happened after he drank the potion or allowing him to leave and do it privately, but warned him of the consequences of observing. Lanyon chose to watch and observed as the figure before him transformed from Hyde into Jekyll, **'like a man restored from death'**. The experience was too much for Lanyon and he died within three weeks.

Lanyon watches Hyde take the potion to change back into Jekyll in a poster for the 1931 film

- Lanyon assumes the role of the narrator.
- Tension is created as it is clear that Lanyon does not know the identity of the messenger, although the reader now does.
- The exact nature of the relationship between Hyde and Jekyll is finally revealed, as well as the nature of Jekyll's scientific work.
- Lanyon explains that Jekyll revealed the science that allowed him to change from one being into another. However, he cannot even begin to think about sharing this with anyone. This neatly allows Stevenson to avoid any attempt at scientific explanation behind such a transformation.
- Lanyon is deliberately chosen for this task by Hyde to gain revenge on his former friend and, in choosing to observe through his own curiosity, Lanyon ruins himself.

Key quotations

Rather, as there was something abnormal and misbegotten in the very essence of the creature that now faced me—something seizing, surprising and revolting—this fresh disparity seemed but to fit in with and to reinforce it; so that to my interest in the man's nature and character, there was added a curiosity as to his origin, his life, his fortune and status in the world. *(Chapter 9)*

"Think before you answer, for it shall be done as you decide. As you decide, you shall be left as you were before, and neither richer nor wiser, unless the sense of service rendered to a man in mortal distress may be counted as a kind of riches of the soul. Or, if you shall so prefer to choose, a new province of knowledge and new avenues to fame and power shall be laid open to you, here, in this room, upon the instant; and your sight shall be blasted by a prodigy to stagger the unbelief of Satan." *(Chapter 9)*

 Activity 6

1. What is the significance of the choice of midnight for the messenger to call on Lanyon?

2. It takes two hours for a locksmith to open the door into the room containing the drawer. What does this **symbolize**?

symbolism using something to represent a concept, idea or theme in a novel

Chapter 10 – Henry Jekyll's Full Statement of the Case

Jekyll's narrative explains that he was born into wealth, established a successful career and became well respected. He quickly realized that his enjoyment of secret, unspecified **'pleasures'** lay at odds with his outward respectability and as a result, he experienced a sense of guilt. Through his scientific studies, he discovered that man is made up of two elements and then set about separating them. He believed that this would free his darker self to enjoy its darker passions without any shame.

Jekyll created a drug that unleashed **'a second form and countenance'**, allowing his darker self to satisfy its primal instincts without consequences. One night he drank the potion. After much pain and a **'horror of the spirit'**, his primitive self was born – younger and stronger, but pure evil. Jekyll was aware of how Hyde repulsed those who saw him, although he delighted in his new form. He used a potion to return to his former self but became increasingly eager to experience life as Hyde for the unrestrained pleasure that it brought.

I LAY DOWN THE PEN, AND PROCEED TO SEAL UP MY CONFESSION

Jekyll writes his confession in an illustration drawn by Edmund J Sullivan for the 1928 publication of the novella

One morning, he woke as Hyde without taking the potion. He found that he was physically bigger than before and it became clear that the evil self was gaining power and taking over his good self. Scared by this experience, he resolved to give it up and return to his former life. However, temptation proved too strong and, two months later, he gave in and, as Hyde, killed Sir Danvers Carew. Again, he resolved to abandon Hyde but found that he was changing into him involuntarily, on one occasion in Regent's Park during daytime. It was then that he called on Lanyon for help and offered him the chance to observe the transformation from Hyde back into Jekyll.

Hyde had become the stronger of the two selves and increased doses of the potion could not deter him. Jekyll reveals that the two selves grew to hate each other and he amended the will, wrote his confession and committed suicide, fearful that he would become Hyde and that the true facts of his life would never be revealed.

- Jekyll takes over the narration through his **'full statement of the case'**. His **confessional account** reveals the answers to the many mysteries of Utterson's and Lanyon's previous narrations.

- He reveals his life history, views on human nature and his creation of a drug to enable him to create his evil **alter ego** – Mr Hyde – which eventually ruins him.

Key quotations

With every day, and from both sides of my intelligence, the moral and the intellectual, I thus drew steadily nearer to that truth, by whose partial discovery I have been doomed to such a dreadful shipwreck: that man is not truly one, but truly two. *(Chapter 10)*

I knew myself, at the first breath of this new life, to be more wicked, tenfold more wicked, sold a slave to my original evil; and the thought, in that moment, braced and delighted me like wine. *(Chapter 10)*

---

alter ego an alternative personality

chronological order the presentation of events in a story in the order in which they actually occurred

confessional form a type of writing in which the characters reveal their innermost thoughts, motivations and actions, so mysteries or secrets are finally revealed

Activity 7

1. It is Hyde's body, not Jekyll's, that is found at the end. What does that say about human nature?

2. Using Jekyll's narrative, create a timeline of events in **chronological order** like the one below.

Jekyll drinks the
potion and turns
into Hyde

Structure

The Strange Case of Dr Jekyll and Mr Hyde is an unusual novel in that it has a **non-linear narrative**, followed by a **linear narrative**. This split successfully reflects the theme of duality that lies at the heart of the novel; the split is also reflected in the use of more than one narrative voice.

The story opens with a **third-person narrative**, centring on Mr Utterson. As such, only what Utterson knows is shared with the reader. Stevenson uses this narrative technique for eight chapters to create and maintain a sense of mystery. As the events do not occur in chronological order, Utterson's sense of confusion about what he participates in is reinforced and suspense is generated.

In Chapter 9, the emphasis shifts to Lanyon's **first-person narrative**. This reveals some answers to the mystery with the intention of keeping the reader in suspense. Chapter 10 is Dr Jekyll's own first-person narrative, written in confessional form, which finally reveals everything. In addressing the reader directly, it also succeeds in creating some sense of sympathy for Jekyll.

The idea of '**testimony**' became established in the 1860s with the emergence of **gothic fiction**. In this **sub-genre**, writers composed their stories around diary entries, letters, confessions, personal manuscripts and official documents. In effect, the reader was presented with a series of inter-related personal documents or 'testimonies'. Each testimony deepened the sense of mystery, presenting a non-linear narrative in which events did not run in chronological order and the narrative voice changed. It was only when put together that the truth was revealed in a climax.

Stevenson's story draws on this tradition with the testimonies of Lanyon and Jekyll and changing narrative voices. The truth is not revealed until the last chapter. The idea of important people revealing their innermost thoughts and experiences is also deliberate. It creates not only a sense of authenticity but also heightens the drama and suspense as the characters speak directly to the reader. Stevenson provides a clue in the title of his work. He presents a 'case', drawing on the tradition of the suburban gothic with its testimony-based content, but he identifies that it is a 'strange' one, alluding to the supernatural forces at work within it.

In your analysis, include words such as 'successfully' and 'effective' in relation to Stevenson's structural choices to show that you are evaluating.

first-person narration a story told from the narrator's point of view, using the pronouns 'I' or 'me'

gothic fiction a literary style characterized by tales of horror and the supernatural

linear narrative the presentation of events in a story in the order in which they actually occurred

non-linear narrative the presentation of events in a story in a different order to that in which they occurred

sub-genre a smaller grouping within a literary genre

testimony a sub-genre of gothic fiction in which a story is told through personal documents like letters or confessions

third-person narration a story told from the perspective of a character or voice outside the story, using the pronouns 'he' and 'she'; this perspective could be limited or it could be 'omniscient' – aware of the thoughts and feelings of all the characters

The novella

The Strange Case of Doctor Jekyll and Mr Hyde is classified as a novella. This is a work of prose fiction that is longer than a short story but shorter than a novel. Ranging from 50 to 100 pages, it has between 20,000 and 50,000 words approximately. It became a recognized literary form in the late 1800s and early 1900s. Famous modern writers of the novella include John Steinbeck, Ernest Hemingway and George Orwell.

Activity 8

1. Talk with a partner about why you think Stevenson chose the novella form for *The Strange Case of Doctor Jekyll and Mr Hyde* and not the short story or novel form.

2. Which famous novellas were written by the authors listed above? Have you read any of these?

Writing about plot and structure

Upgrade

The starting point for success is having an excellent knowledge and understanding of the whole plot. Even though you may not be asked a question about plot specifically, it underpins everything else you will be questioned on. There is no substitute for knowing the text so well that you can adapt and tailor your knowledge and understanding to the question you answer. This doesn't mean retelling the story; instead you should select the information that is relevant to the question.

You will also need to know about structure, showing an understanding of how Stevenson has chosen to shape his novel in order to communicate his ideas to the reader.

Biography of Robert Louis Stevenson

- 1818 – Mary Shelley's *Frankenstein* is published.
- 1837 – Queen Victoria succeeds William IV.
- 1850 – Robert Louis Stevenson is born in Edinburgh, Scotland.
- 1859 – *The Origin of the Species* by Charles Darwin is published.
- 1861 – Stevenson attends Edinburgh Academy.
- 1867 – Stevenson studies engineering at Edinburgh University.
- 1871 – Stevenson decides to study law.
- 1873 – Stevenson and his father argue when he announces he does not believe in Christianity. He travels to the French Riviera because the warmer climate helps his tuberculosis.
- 1875 – Stevenson passes his final law exams but does not practise. He travels to France.
- 1876 – He meets Fanny Osbourne, an American who is married with children.
- 1878 – He publishes *Edinburgh Picturesque* and *An Inland Voyage*.
- 1879 – He travels to America.
- 1880 – Stevenson marries Fanny in California. He returns to Scotland and writes *Deacon Brodie*, a play, with a central figure who has a double personality. He leaves for Switzerland.
- 1882 – Stevenson moves to France.
- 1883 – *Treasure Island* is published.
- 1884 – He returns to England seriously ill and publishes *The Body Snatcher* and *Markheim*, two short stories.
- 1885 – He writes *The Strange Case of Dr Jekyll and Mr Hyde*.
- 1886 – He publishes *The Strange Case of Dr Jekyll and Mr Hyde* and *Kidnapped*.
- 1887 – Stevenson goes to America following the death of his father.
- 1888 – He leaves America and then takes a cruise to the South Pacific.
- 1889 – He starts life in Samoa and publishes *The Master of Ballantrae*.
- 1890 – He cruises to Australia and New Zealand before returning to Samoa.
- 1894 – Stevenson dies in Samoa, aged 44.
- 1900 – Freud publishes *Interpretation of Dreams*.
- 1901 – Queen Victoria dies.

Robert Louis Stevenson (1850–1894) is one of the most translated authors in the world

Historical and cultural context of the novel

Victorian England

The era gets its name from the reign of Queen Victoria, which began in 1837 and ended in 1901. It was a time of unprecedented change, as Great Britain transformed during the Industrial Revolution from an agricultural economy to an industrial one. Great Britain also became the world's superpower in both financial and military terms. It is estimated that England ruled one fifth of the globe at this time, prompting the phrase 'the sun never sets on the British Empire'.

The period has two distinct phases. What successfully changed Great Britain in the early part of Victoria's reign later caused huge social problems in the second half. Stevenson wrote his book during this later period when there was much criticism of, and dissatisfaction with, politics, religion and daily life.

Key facts about Victorian England

- A huge movement of people from the country into the major cities like London and Glasgow took place. This resulted in a massive growth in the population, from 13.8 million in 1831 to 32.5 million in 1901.

- Transport systems were developed with the expansion of the rail network as well as the development of ports and use of steamships. This meant goods and people could be moved about more freely and quickly. The London Underground was created.

- Communication was enhanced by improvements to the postal network and the development of telegraph and telephone.

- All of the above facilitated increased trade and commerce not only within Britain but with other countries, establishing it as the world's financial centre.

- In medicine, chloroform became widely used as an anaesthetic in dentistry and surgery. Carbolic acid was used as an antiseptic.

- Progress was made in sanitation with the development of a sewage system in London.

Key facts about Victorian England

- Other improvements in the standard of living saw the development of water and gas networks.

- Many of these developments were essential as England and Great Britain tried to cope with the massive, and sometimes too speedy, transformation into a modern, industrialized nation. Living conditions for the poorest were appalling and disease, especially tuberculosis, was widespread.

- The period is also known for many other social ills such as poverty, child labour, abuse of alcohol and drugs, and widespread prostitution. It is estimated that there were approximately 80,000 prostitutes in London in the 1850s.

- Great Britain also found itself facing foreign conflicts as some of its colonies revolted in the second half of Queen Victoria's rule.

The poor crowded into Victorian London and lived in squalid, unhealthy conditions (*A Busy Scene on London Bridge* by Gustave Doré, 1872)

Activity 1

Research the following: Pax Britannica, 'Penny Black', Great Exhibition of 1851, Isambard Kingdom Brunel and the Boer War. What would you identify as the top five key points about each of these?

The Victorian compromise

The most popular and stereotypical image of Victorian England is the one of serious, excessively polite men and women standing in drawing rooms discussing the important issues of the day. The playing of a sober piano piece is the usual form of entertainment portrayed. The reality though is very different. The Victorians were actually regular thrill seekers.

Key facts about Victorian England

- The Victorians were responsible for what we now call holidays, as working hours, particularly for the middle classes, became more structured and the idea of leisure time arose.

- They had an appetite for scandal and were avid readers of publications that provided gossip and talk of contemporary celebrities. *The News of the World* was first published in 1843.

- The Victorians were cinema-goers and gamblers.

- Thrilling, dangerous and daringly spectacular stage shows were very popular, as were freak shows.

- With colonies in the West Indies, the Victorians were soon enjoying curry dishes.

- The Victorian appetite for drugs was incredible. Laudanum, a mixture of opium and alcohol, was the drug of choice. It was freely available and widely used across all social classes. Gin was a popular drink, which was consumed in 'gin palaces'.

Much of polite Victorian society was oblivious to the plight of the poorest people or the seedier side of life (*The Bayswater Omnibus* by George William Joy, 1895)

This lifestyle coexisted alongside a strict moral code by which society was expected to live. This promoted church attendance, good manners, academic achievement and professional employment, family values, charity and the highest moral values. Obviously, this required the first kind of behaviour being kept secret in order to preserve the second. This is known as 'the Victorian compromise', or the ability of middle- and upper-class Victorian society to indulge their wilder desires but maintain their outwardly respectable appearance. It is clear that Stevenson criticizes this idea in his novella.

Activity 2

Find supporting quotations from the beginning of Chapter 10 to support the idea of the Victorian compromise.

Knowing about and appreciating the social, historical and cultural contexts in which a novel was written will improve and enrich your understanding of it. However, only mention context in relation to your exam question when relevant.

Colonialism

Queen Victoria ruled over India, Australia, Canada, New Zealand, South Africa, Rhodesia (now Zimbabwe), Hong Kong, Gibraltar, several islands in the West Indies and colonies on the African coast. In 1899, English poet Rudyard Kipling published a poem called 'The White Man's Burden', which caused controversy. Some viewed it as a positive message persuading the western world to support the developing world. Others, however, saw it as an arrogant statement of superiority by western Europeans, proclaiming their right to rule over the 'less civilized', un-Christian, 'wild' natives of the undeveloped world.

Although Stevenson's death was some years before the poem's publication, colonialism is an important contextual influence because the Victorians were extremely enthusiastic in their support of colonial expansion and proud of their achievements. They felt superior to the indigenous peoples in their colonies and believed they were doing the work of God in 'civilizing' them. This was despite their secretive use of drugs, excessive gambling and drinking, use of prostitutes and exploitation of child labour. Some critics interpret Stevenson's work as an attack on this hypocrisy.

Education

Education in Victorian England differed depending on gender and class. The upper classes educated their children at home until the boys could attend the elite, private schools of the time such as Eton, before entering an elite university. Girls were also educated at home but did not progress to university. The less wealthy had access to education too. Approximately 200 'ragged schools' provided education free of charge for the very poorest families in Great Britain. Trade unions became required by law to ensure three hours of schooling a day for 'workhouse' children and the 1870 Education Act resulted in the government providing funding for certain schools.

The curriculum was based on the three 'Rs' – reading, writing and arithmetic. Religion and Bible study featured heavily too. Some critics interpret Stevenson's portrayal of Jekyll as a warning of the dangers of too much knowledge.

Religion and science

At the beginning of the 19th century, church attendance was strong. The Church of England dominated. It was wealthy and a powerful influence across all aspects of society. Success was seen to be the result of a virtuous life, while failure suggested a life of vice. Religious leaders explained the relationship between God and science through the theory of intelligent design. The natural world was interpreted and promoted as evidence of an ultimate designer – God.

However, the power of religion was under threat during the later stages of the era. The Industrial Revolution and the rapid changes it brought about meant that more educated people were ready to question the religious doctrine they had been taught. There was also greater awareness of new thinking from abroad. Darwin's *The Origin of Species* provided a serious alternative to accepted thinking. The fruits of the Industrial Revolution were evident during the Victorian era when the age of modern invention was born. Science not only improved daily life but challenged the established, religious thinking of the time and the powerful hold that organized religious institutions had on the people.

Key facts: Charles Darwin

Charles Darwin was an English naturalist, who published *The Origin of Species* in 1859. This publication challenged the creation myth found in the Book of Genesis in the Bible, explaining man's evolution in scientific terms. Darwin argued that humans resulted from a process of natural selection, essentially survival of the fittest. His theory was well received, supported as it was by convincing evidence. In offering an alternative version for the development of mankind to the received religious thinking of the time, it created a huge impact and tension between religion and science.

Satirical engraving entitled 'The Lion of the Season', 1861, when controversy over Darwin's theories in *The Origin of Species* was raging

Activity 3

Select the correct word from below to complete the text, which explains how *The Origin of Species* relates to *The Strange Case of Dr Jekyll and Mr Hyde*.

- interpreted
- conflict
- evolution
- scientific
- challenged

Stevenson _____ the accepted idea that God and God alone is responsible for the creation of mankind. This _____ between the religious and the scientific was already in existence following the publication of Darwin's 'The Origin of Species' in 1859, which put forward the theory of _____. In this context, Jekyll can be _____ as an alternative to God as he creates another man, Mr Hyde. Jekyll's alter ego is the result of a process that can be explained and supported by _____ theory, although the novella never explicitly does this.

Freud and psychology

There was much interest in the mind and how it worked during the Victorian period, especially in the later stages. Sigmund Freud was a psychoanalyst, who built on the work of earlier neurologists. He put forward the idea that man pushed his most disturbing and unacceptable ideas and desires far from his consciousness, into his unconscious mind. These repressed ideas could be released, according to Freud, through various techniques such as dream analysis, hypnosis and especially psychoanalysis. This approach involved a highly trained therapist drawing out these unconscious thoughts and ideas from the individual through intense conversations over a period of time. Freud's 1900 publication

Sigmund Freud (1856–1939) is considered to be the founding father of psychoanalysis

Interpretation of Dreams emphasized that these suppressed desires were often sexual in nature. Although published after Stevenson's death, it is probable that he was aware of these ideas and theories. Some critics argue that Hyde is the embodiment of Jekyll's repressed desires.

Activity 4

Write a paragraph explaining how Freud's theory of repressed desires could relate to *The Strange Case of Dr Jekyll and Mr Hyde*.

Consider which character or characters best exemplify 'repressed desires' and how this is represented in the novella. Do any characters other than the protagonists hint at repressed desires?

Horror fiction and the gothic

Horror or fantasy fiction developed out of folklore, legend and religious traditions. It targets the fear of death, the unknown, evil and the devil with stories of witches and werewolves, ghosts and ghouls. The purpose is to cause an emotional reaction in the reader, be it terror or horror. Terror is defined as the fear of what is about to happen, while horror is classified as revulsion at what has happened. In this context, horror fiction moved away from depending only on the supernatural or the fantastic and began to involve the normal and the ordinary.

Gothic fiction combined elements of horror and romance and came to prominence as a genre in Europe in the 1800s. Henry Walpole's *The Castle of Otranto* is seen as the first essentially gothic work of fiction and the genre takes its name from its subtitle, *'A Gothic Work'*. Such works place an emphasis on mystery, supernatural forces, strange settings and suspense. Powerful secrets often lie at the heart of these novels. Traditionally, these stories were set in the Europe of the Middle Ages but, as the genre developed, authors began to set their novels in more recognizable places and also developed their characters as more recognizable. The intention was to increase the fear of the reader. Stevenson draws on this approach, presenting characters and settings that were instantly recognizable to his contemporary audience alongside supernatural elements. This intensified the experience for the Victorian reader, who was faced with an instantly familiar world, which was suddenly equally frightening.

The genre was a reaction to the emphasis on reason and the stifling of emotions, which dominated Victorian life. It served as a warning that the rational alone could not explain the world around us. Although these works challenged conventional thinking, they also served as a warning as the heroes often died in the end. The pursuit of knowledge and the challenging of accepted scientific and moral boundaries was seen to cause ruin and downfall.

Bela Lugosi taking the lead role in the 1931 film, *Dracula*, in typically gothic style

Activity 5

Complete the table below, identifying how Stevenson includes each of the listed conventions of the gothic genre in his novella.

Gothic convention	Example from *The Strange Case of Dr Jekyll and Mr Hyde*
Mysterious and sinister buildings	
Labyrinthine passages	
Shadows, darkness, flickering candlelight	
Extreme weather conditions	
Secrets	
Central figure who pushes the boundaries and ruins himself	
Supernatural forces at work	
Terrifying events	
True identities revealed at the end	

Writing about context

Upgrade

You may not be directly assessed on social and historical context. However, this does not mean that you should not research the background to the novella – simply that it will not be included in your question.

An author's work is influenced by what is happening and being thought about at the time of writing. It is important to understand and appreciate that books are often a product of their time. Your understanding and enjoyment of the novella will be better as a result.

Main characters

Dr Henry Jekyll

Jekyll is a well-respected and successful scientist, good friend of Mr Utterson and former friend of Dr Lanyon. Hyde is his alter ego. Jekyll confesses all in the final chapter of the novella, bringing this 'strange case' to its conclusion.

The reader is first introduced to Jekyll in Chapter 3. By this stage, an air of mystery about him has already been established, arising from his relationship with Hyde. Utterson suspects Hyde is blackmailing Jekyll and may even attempt to kill him in order to inherit from his will. Jekyll is initially presented as sociable, throwing a dinner party for friends – all reputable Victorian gentlemen. Physically, he is described as healthy, strong and handsome. He is close to Utterson, for whom he holds a sincere and warm affection. Less positively, he is critical of his former friend, Dr Lanyon, describing him repeatedly as **"a hide-bound pedant"** *(Chapter 3)*, in whom he is disappointed.

Jekyll admits to a certain vanity, **'fond of the respect of the wise and good among my fellow-men'** *(Chapter 10)*, which clashes with his **'impatient gaiety of disposition'** *(Chapter 10)*, leading him to conceal his pleasures. This results in what he calls **'a profound duplicity of life'** *(Chapter 10)*; at times he is **'plunged in shame'** *(Chapter 10)* but at other times he works hard **'at the furtherance of knowledge or the relief of sorrow and suffering'** *(Chapter 10)*. The specific details of his shameful and guilty activities are never revealed but it is clear that Stevenson is using Jekyll to represent the hypocrisy of Victorian society, which uses its superficially respectable outward face to mask a darker, more sinister appetite. Jekyll identifies this when he says that **'man is not truly one, but truly two'** *(Chapter 10)*; the duality of man and the separation of good and bad in the individual becomes the focus of his scientific work. This work remains incomplete, but Jekyll creates a drug that unleashes his purely evil side. It is important to remember, however, that while Hyde is completely evil, Jekyll remains a mixture of good and bad, so their personalities are not just good vs. evil.

Jekyll's selfishness in his actions is clear. He makes careful preparations so that he can **'profit by the strange immunities'** *(Chapter 10)* of his position. He revels in the thought of enjoying his pleasures, feeling that he is outside society and the law, and celebrates the fact that his **'safety was complete'** *(Chapter 10)*. He buys and furnishes a house in Soho for Hyde, complete with a silent, unscrupulous housekeeper. His own servants are ordered to ensure that Hyde has full access at his own residence and his will is drawn up so that Hyde inherits everything if anything happens to Jekyll. He thinks he has it all, until he realizes that Hyde seeks out not just the undignified but the monstrous, malign and villainous. He admits that **'his conscience slumbered'** *(Chapter 10)*, neatly excusing himself from wrong, saying it was **'Hyde alone, that was guilty'** *(Chapter 10)*. He then goes further following the incident with the young girl by opening a bank account for Hyde and forging his signature to protect Hyde and himself from detection.

Things deteriorate and Jekyll admits to 'losing hold of my original and better self' *(Chapter 10)*. He states that whereas 'in the beginning, the difficulty has been to throw off the body of Jekyll, it had of late, gradually but decidedly transferred itself to the other side' *(Chapter 10)*. Increased doses of the potion are needed to manage the situation. When Jekyll wakes up one morning as Hyde, he decides to try to abandon his other self completely, which he manages for two months. However, Jekyll cannot resist the temptation and in a moment of weakness takes the drug that transforms him into Hyde. The returning Hyde is all the more murderous and depraved, killing Sir Danvers with an unparalleled ferocity, 'tasting delight from every blow' *(Chapter 10)*. This event prompts Jekyll to abandon Hyde again, but it is too late, as he realizes when he involuntarily transforms into Hyde while sitting in Regent's Park.

Jekyll's remaining days are a battle between his two selves with Hyde uncontrollable and the transformative drug no longer available despite Jekyll's frantic and desperate searches for it. He reflects that the whole process must have been possible only because the very first chemical he used was impure. Jekyll's health declines, worn out by the unpredictable appearances of Hyde and the hate that now divides the two selves. His last desperate act is suicide and he dies not knowing if Hyde will reappear or escape.

Jekyll mixes potions in the 1941 film starring Spencer Tracey

Activity 1

1. Reread the description of the first time Jekyll changes into Hyde in Chapter 10, from 'I hesitated long before…' to '… I had lost in stature.' How does Stevenson make this passage dramatic?

2. Find a quotation at the start of Chapter 2 that gives a physical description of Jekyll suggesting his darker side. Explore its significance.

3. Jekyll is an **overreacher**, someone who pushes the boundaries of science in his quest for knowledge, and is ruined as a result. Research the character of Victor Frankenstein in Mary Shelley's novel *Frankenstein*. He is also an overreacher. What similarities are there between Jekyll and Victor Frankenstein?

4. Imagine that Jekyll has a Twitter account. Using the last chapter, write 15–20 tweets for Jekyll to explain his thoughts and feelings. Each tweet should be no more than 140 characters in length.

overreacher someone who pushes the boundaries of science in their quest for knowledge and is ruined as a result

Make sure that you support your comments and analysis of characters with carefully selected quotations from the novella. These should be short – ideally no longer than one sentence.

This poster, advertising an early dramatization of the novella, depicts the transformation of the upright, gentlemanly Jekyll into the lowly, monstrous Hyde

Mr Edward Hyde

Hyde is Jekyll's alter ego and the result of Jekyll's attempts to separate the good and evil sides of his nature. Hyde is the embodiment of the dark side of the scientist's nature: pure evil in human form. In Chapter 10, the moment of transformation is described as **'a grinding in the bones, deadly nausea, and a horror of the spirit that cannot be exceeded at the hour of birth or death'**; Jekyll welcomes the change, confessing to a **'heady recklessness'** that **'delighted me like wine'**.

Hyde is smaller than Jekyll but in this form he feels younger, lighter and happier. In Chapter 10, he suggests that the smaller figure is the result of **'nine tenths a life of effort, virtue and control'** and because Jekyll's unrestrained evil **'had been much less exercised and much less exhausted'**. He admits that Hyde's body has an element of deformity and decay but he has no sense of disgust at what he has become and instead welcomes it. Hyde enables Jekyll to satisfy his more sinister self and his undignified urges without any hint of shame or guilt.

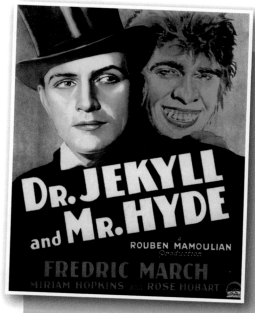

Jekyll is shadowed by his alter ego Hyde in a poster for the 1931 film

These urges, however, soon give way to Hyde's much more monstrous activities and Jekyll describes Hyde as **'inherently malign and villainous'** *(Chapter 10)*. He exempts himself from blame, saying that the guilt is all Hyde's, and so his **'conscience slumbered'** *(Chapter 10)*. The casual assault of the young child and the murder of Sir Danvers Carew are two examples of Hyde's capacity for depravity and violence.

There are frequent references to Hyde's animalistic nature. For example, he is described as being ape-like by the maid who witnesses him kill Sir Danvers Carew; Poole notices that he moves like a monkey; Utterson detects a **'hissing intake of the breath'** *(Chapter 2)*, which implies a snakelike quality and also identifies his savage laugh; later Poole also recalls a **'dismal screech, as of mere animal terror'** *(Chapter 8)* coming from Hyde (which might give us a brief moment of sympathy for him). To Utterson, he is hardly human.

There is universal disgust from those who meet Hyde. Enfield identifies **"something downright detestable"** *(Chapter 1)* in him while Utterson is also filled with disgust, loathing and fear on meeting him. Jekyll is aware of this, but is unconcerned. More importantly, characters feel a deep sense of unease when they meet Hyde, which they are unable to explain. Poole and Enfield both note this, but Utterson summarizes their views when he says, **'Only on one point, were they agreed; and that was the haunting sense of unexpected deformity with which the fugitive impressed his beholders'** *(Chapter 4)*. The confusion these characters feel may come from Hyde's contradictory nature. He possesses **'a sort of murderous mixture of timidity and boldness'** *(Chapter 2)* and according to Lanyon there is a **'remarkable combination of great muscular activity and great apparent debility of constitution'** *(Chapter 9)*. It is actually Jekyll himself who provides the answer when he explains that **'Hyde, alone in the ranks of mankind, was pure evil'** *(Chapter 10)*. This is then reinforced through references to Hyde as a devil. Utterson can read **"Satan's signature"** *(Chapter 2)* in Hyde's face and Enfield describes him as being really like Satan.

Jekyll's master plan – to do as he pleases, free of guilt and shame as well as from the reaches of the law – backfires in spectacular fashion. Hyde grows in power and force. Attempts to resist him prove futile for his force is so strong that on one occasion Jekyll goes to bed as himself but, to his horror, wakes up as Hyde. As Hyde's force grows, so he does physically and, despite Jekyll's best efforts, he cannot easily be suppressed by drugs or potions. The Hyde who so viciously murders Sir Danvers Carew is, according to Jekyll, even more evil because Jekyll tried to abandon him for two months.

One day, as Jekyll sits in Regent's Park, he suddenly transforms. Hyde is full of **'inordinate anger, strung to the pitch of murder, lusting to inflict pain'** *(Chapter 10)*. Despite this he is also sharp mentally and it is this Hyde who formulates the plan to ruin Lanyon. The involuntary transformation into Hyde

Hyde's murderous nature is highlighted in this still from the 1919 film

happens regularly at all hours and, as Hyde grows in strength, Jekyll weakens. Jekyll's narrative also reveals how the two divided selves grow to hate each other, with Hyde destroying Jekyll's father's letters and portrait to spite him. However, Jekyll still feels pity for the evil being he created because of Hyde's love of life and deep-seated terror at being killed through Jekyll's suicide.

In Hyde, Stevenson creates a metaphor for the less publically acceptable and sometimes immoral and illegal behaviour in Victorian society. Hyde represents the evil that lurked beneath the façade of respectability and decorum at the time of writing and which, the novella suggests, lurks in everyone. It is worth noting that Stevenson decides that Jekyll will transform into Hyde even as he lies dying, so it is this side of his nature that finally is found by Utterson and Poole, not the respected scientist.

In your answer, it is important that you show how Stevenson deliberately uses the characters he creates to represent or express important ideas. Very often, a character represents a specific theme or point of view.

Activity 2

1. Reread the incident where Hyde tramples over the young girl in Chapter 1. Complete the table to analyse how Stevenson emphasizes Hyde's evil.

Quotation	Language device	Effect
'stumping'	emotive verb	This suggests that he walked forcefully in an aggressive manner.
'calmly'		
'it was hellish'		
'it was like some damned Juggernaught'		

2. Now write a paragraph, using the ideas above, to analyse Stevenson's use of language to emphasize Hyde's evil nature.

3. Reread the episode of Sir Danvers Carew's murder in Chapter 4. How does Stevenson use language here to emphasize Hyde's terrible violence during this episode?

4. Make a note of all references to Hyde as a devil or being from hell throughout the novella.

5. Write a paragraph explaining the significance of the fact that it is Hyde's dead body that Utterson and Poole find, not Jekyll's.

Mr Gabriel Utterson

Utterson is the main narrator. Like the reader, his knowledge and understanding of events is limited and imperfect, crucial to the success of the novella. A lawyer by profession, he is presented as well-respected and successful, with Sir Danvers Carew, a member of parliament, among his clientele. As a lawyer, he is good at keeping secrets and confidences, and is ashamed of himself when he feels he may be gossiping. Loyalty is important to him and his many friendships are formed with relatives or those he has known the longest, including Lanyon and Jekyll. By nature, he is a dispassionate man, described as undemonstrative, who is almost envious of the high jinks and escapades of others. He is 'a lover of the sane and customary sides of life, to whom the fanciful was the immodest' *(Chapter 2)*. This is all very deliberate on the part of Stevenson who presents us with a man of common sense, at the heart of a supernatural tale, who will not sensationalize the already sensational and fantastic events he uncovers.

Utterson is first described in Chapter 1 as an odd mixture of positive and negative. He is 'embarrassed in discourse' despite being a lawyer, which demands articulate, well-developed public speaking skills. Although 'lean, long, dusty, dreary' and with a face which was 'never lighted by a smile', he is also described as 'lovable'. His weekly walks with his distant cousin Enfield reinforce his contradictory nature, for while they are important to Utterson and something he would not miss, the two men speak very little, making the reader wonder what pleasure they gain from their walks. While 'austere with himself' *(Chapter 1)*, Utterson has 'an approved tolerance for other' *(Chapter 1)* and his non-judgemental nature goes some way to explaining why he does not take action when fears about Jekyll's behaviour, as protector of a murderer, are raised.

Like Lanyon, Utterson is a rational and logical man. He initially criticizes Poole for his theory that Hyde has murdered Jekyll as 'it doesn't commend itself to reason' *(Chapter 8)*. There is no place for the unconventional or supernatural in his world. His encounter with Hyde leaves him feeling confused as he attempts to rationalize the experience. While noting Hyde's many unpleasant features, Utterson is struck by the fact that 'not all of these together could explain the hitherto unknown disgust, loathing and fear' *(Chapter 2)* that he feels. He muses further that "There *is* something more, if I could find a name for it" *(Chapter 2)*. This quest is pointless because Utterson cannot imagine the supernatural and otherworldly truth. Note how he attempts rather desperately to convince Poole that the creature in the room must be Jekyll, citing "one of those maladies that both torture and deform the sufferer" *(Chapter 8)*. When confronted by the changing expression on Jekyll's face at the window, Utterson is reduced to silence because he cannot make sense of the supernatural.

Utterson represents the Victorian gentleman. He is educated, respectable, professional, polite and dignified. In his first encounter with Hyde, he is critical of his own language, which he says is "not fitting" *(Chapter 2)*. When confronted by

Jekyll's terrified servants, he is unhappy that they are not behaving as servants should. Rules and customs matter to him, as do reputations and opinions. Although the situation frequently demands action, Utterson is more concerned with protecting Jekyll's reputation from **"the cancer of some concealed disgrace"** *(Chapter 2)* and further scandal. In this context, he is very much a **metaphor** for Victorian society's obsession with maintaining reputation. Utterson reflects on what secrets may lurk in Jekyll's past and imagines that Hyde too **"must have secrets of his own: black secrets"** *(Chapter 2)*. All of these remain unrevealed and secrecy permeates the whole novella, as indeed it did the whole of Victorian society, as the outward, respectable face hid more sinister realities. This darkness is hinted at in Utterson's dream, which represents his unconscious reality, so different from his dominant rational self. Utterson himself recognizes the two sides of his world when he admits how Hyde **'touched him on the intellectual side alone; but now his imagination also was engaged or rather enslaved'** *(Chapter 2)*. What follows is a nightmare in which a faceless figure, presumably Hyde, rampages through the streets of London trampling over defenceless children and threatening Jekyll. It is this experience – a rare departure from the logical, rational world – which creates Utterson's desire to see Hyde.

> **metaphor** a comparison of one thing to another to make a description more vivid; a metaphor states that one thing *is* the other

Activity 3

1. Write a paragraph analysing your first impressions of Utterson, using the words below and carefully selected quotations to support your points.

   - portrayal
   - trustworthy
   - contradictory
   - non-judgemental
   - unexciting
   - loyal

2. Create a page for Utterson to go on a social networking site. How will you reflect his personality and nature?

3. Think about the names given to the characters. Are these significant?

Avoid simply retelling what characters in the novel say or do. To read with insight and analysis, and gain better marks, you must think about *how* what characters say and do reveals their personalities and natures.

Dr Hastie Lanyon

Lanyon first appears in Chapter 2, when Utterson visits to ask him for information about Hyde. When he appears again in Chapter 6, Utterson is shocked at the state he finds him in, which the reader discovers later is the result of having watched Hyde transform back into Jekyll. Lanyon then provides the narration of Chapter 9, although already dead, through his letter to Utterson in which he reveals his attempts to help Jekyll and the reasons for his own sudden decline and resulting death.

Lanyon is a well-respected and successful doctor. Chapter 2 reveals a lot about his relationships with Utterson and Jekyll. His friendship with Utterson goes back to when they were both 'old mates both at school and college' (Chapter 2). They are 'thorough respecters of [...] each other' (Chapter 2) who also enjoy each other's company. They share similar interests and values as well as a common friend in Jekyll. However, a tension is established early on when Lanyon confesses that he sees little of Jekyll, despite what Utterson calls, 'a bond of common interest' (their profession) (Chapter 2). It is "more than ten years since Henry Jekyll became too fanciful" (Chapter 2) for Lanyon, who feels his former close friend went "wrong in mind" (Chapter 2). Lanyon is scathing of Jekyll's "unscientific balderdash" (Chapter 2) and discussion of this difficult topic causes him to become very angry. He is in professional opposition to Jekyll's ideas and methodologies, and is clearly identified as a man of traditional and rational beliefs.

The description of Lanyon in Chapter 6 contrasts greatly with that in Chapter 2. Whereas before he was 'a hearty, healthy, dapper, red-faced gentleman, with a shock of hair' (Chapter 2), he is now pale, drawn, visibly balder and older. The difference could not be more striking. Having witnessed Hyde's transformation, the formerly boisterous and theatrical Lanyon is now a nervous and shrunken wreck, gladly awaiting death. Utterson notices a deep-rooted terror in his friend and mistakenly believes Utterson knows he has a terminal illness, ironically stating: "the knowledge is more than he can bear" (Chapter 6).

It is true that Lanyon has learned something that has overpowered and destroyed him. However, it is not related to his own health, but the sight of Hyde as his features 'seemed to melt and alter' (Chapter 9) becoming Jekyll. It is a vision that forces him to react with horror and terror. This phenomena shatters Lanyon's views and understanding of the world. Although he listens to Jekyll for an hour and sees the theory in action, even as a scientist Lanyon is unable to accept or believe what has happened. This could be interpreted as Lanyon failing to accept the darker aspects of his own nature. Knowledge and its pursuit has been his profession and now it is his ruin, as he admits "if we knew all, we should be more glad to get away" (Chapter 6).

It is important to note, however, that Lanyon plays a very significant role in his own downfall. While it is clear that he is deliberately targeted by Hyde's scheme and feels a sense of duty to help a former close friend, it is equally clear that his decision to observe Hyde change back into Jekyll is completely his own. Hyde's offer is an honest one, warning that he will be **"blasted by a prodigy to stagger the unbelief of Satan"** *(Chapter 9)* and yet Lanyon chooses to watch, cynically stating that he has gone too far to turn back. Hyde himself identifies **"greed of curiosity"** *(Chapter 9)* as Lanyon's motivation. The outcome – Lanyon's ruin – is absolute. As he says, he will never recover and nothing can be done to prevent his death.

Activity 4

1. Reread the description of the place where Lanyon lives and how Utterson refers to his friend in Chapter 2. How does this create the impression of a knowledgeable and important man?

2. What does the phrase "wrong in mind" suggest about what Lanyon believes happened to Jekyll?

3. Do some research into Damon and Pythias, the two characters from Greek mythology referred to by Lanyon. Could this reference suggest anything about his friendship with Jekyll?

4. Reread the description of Hyde changing back into Jekyll in Chapter 9, starting from 'A cry followed…' to '… my mind submerged in terror'. Why is this written in one long sentence?

5. Complete the table below to analyse the language used at the end of Chapter 9 to describe the effect of Hyde's transformation on Lanyon's life. Add more quotations to the table.

Quotation	Language device	Effect
'My life is shaken to its roots'	personification	This suggests that Lanyon's understanding of the world is revealed to be completely wrong. With the foundations of his understanding removed, he cannot function.
'sleep has left me'		
'the deadliest terror sits by me at all hours of the day'		

6. Write a paragraph analysing how Stevenson's use of language reinforces the dreadful impact that Lanyon's experience has had on his life.

Character summary

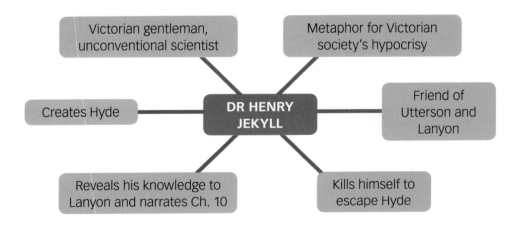

DR HENRY JEKYLL

- Victorian gentleman, unconventional scientist
- Metaphor for Victorian society's hypocrisy
- Creates Hyde
- Friend of Utterson and Lanyon
- Reveals his knowledge to Lanyon and narrates Ch. 10
- Kills himself to escape Hyde

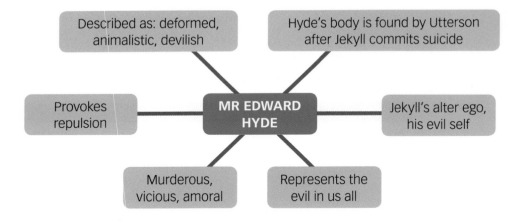

MR EDWARD HYDE

- Described as: deformed, animalistic, devilish
- Hyde's body is found by Utterson after Jekyll commits suicide
- Provokes repulsion
- Jekyll's alter ego, his evil self
- Murderous, vicious, amoral
- Represents the evil in us all

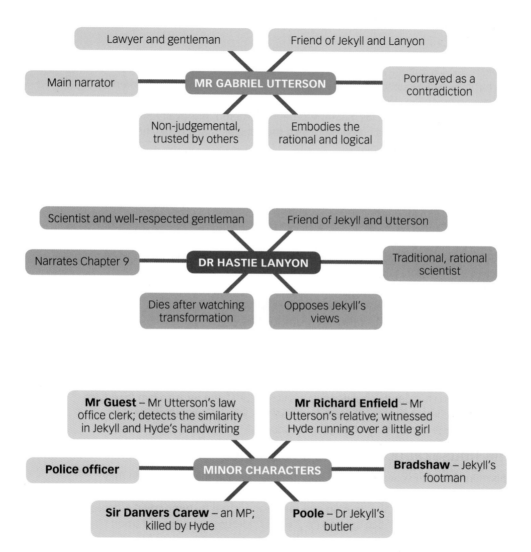

Lawyer and gentleman

Friend of Jekyll and Lanyon

Main narrator

MR GABRIEL UTTERSON

Portrayed as a contradiction

Non-judgemental, trusted by others

Embodies the rational and logical

Scientist and well-respected gentleman

Friend of Jekyll and Utterson

Narrates Chapter 9

DR HASTIE LANYON

Traditional, rational scientist

Dies after watching transformation

Opposes Jekyll's views

Mr Guest – Mr Utterson's law office clerk; detects the similarity in Jekyll and Hyde's handwriting

Mr Richard Enfield – Mr Utterson's relative; witnessed Hyde running over a little girl

Police officer

MINOR CHARACTERS

Bradshaw – Jekyll's footman

Sir Danvers Carew – an MP; killed by Hyde

Poole – Dr Jekyll's butler

Minor characters

Poole

Poole is Jekyll's butler, who diligently carries out his duties and his master's increasingly odd requests. He shows that he is an independent thinker when he decides to persuade Utterson to uncover the identity of the person locked away in Jekyll's room, fearing that his master has been murdered. His loyalty and concern for Jekyll is clear and he is prepared to face the dangers that lurk behind the door to see if there has been foul play.

Mr Richard Enfield

Enfield is Utterson's distant relation, a well-know man about town who accompanies him on his weekly walks. In relating the story of Hyde trampling over the young girl, he is the first to mention Jekyll's alter ego. He is, no doubt, a gentleman with a good profession and reputation, although where he was coming from at 'three o'clock of a black winter morning' *(Chapter 1)* is not revealed.

Bradshaw

Jekyll's footman Bradshaw is called to support Utterson and Poole as they break down the door in Chapter 9. He is instructed to wait by the rear entrance of the laboratory in case the unidentified creature tries to escape via this route.

Mr Guest

Utterson's head clerk, Mr Guest, is something of a handwriting expert. Utterson reveals that he frequently confides secrets in Mr Guest and turns to him for advice regarding the letter supposedly sent from Hyde to Jekyll. Guest identifies the similarity in the handwriting of Jekyll and Hyde.

The housekeeper at Hyde's residence

This elderly housekeeper opens the door to Utterson and the police when they visit Hyde's Soho residence after the murder of Sir Danvers Carew. Although she has excellent manners, she 'had an evil face, smoothed by hypocrisy' *(Chapter 4)*. She is portrayed as mean-spirited ('A flash of odious joy appeared upon the woman's face' *(Chapter 4)*) and nosey ("he is in trouble! What has he done?" *(Chapter 4)*).

Police officer

He visits Utterson to inform him of the murder of Sir Danvers Carew. When the victim's identity is confirmed as an MP, 'his eye lighted up with professional ambition' *(Chapter 4)*. In portraying his motivation as personal gain rather than the pursuit of justice, Stevenson criticizes the hypocrisy at the heart of the Victorian establishment.

Writing about character

Upgrade

An understanding of the characters of *The Strange Case of Dr Jekyll and Mr Hyde* is essential. You will need to analyse the characters and what they represent, and carefully select quotations to support your views about the text. For example, you could say that Hyde is a metaphor for the evil that lurked within Victorian society:

> Hyde is evil in pure form. He is not only the evil unleashed from within Jekyll but is best interpreted as a metaphor for the evil that lurked below the surface respectability of Victorian society. This is successfully conveyed when Jekyll says, 'I was the first that could thus plod in the public eye with a load of genial respectability, and in a moment, like a school boy, strip off these lendings and spring headlong into the sea of liberty.'

You will also need to identify and then analyse how the language features used by the writer affect the reader, explaining if you find them successful or not. Using the quotation above, you could do this in the following way:

> Jekyll makes clear how he finds his outward respectability, although very important to him, boring. He uses the verb 'plod' to suggest that this side of his life lacks excitement and the thrilling pace of one immoral activity followed by another. He uses the basic but effective simile 'like a school boy' to suggest his giddiness at the prospect of being able to satisfy his darker desires. The metaphor, 'spring headlong into the sea of liberty' successfully suggests the eagerness and enthusiasm with which he commits himself to this side of his life. The point is reinforced with alliteration.

Language

The language of the novella

Language is not static. It is constantly changing and evolving. Stevenson wrote his novella more than a century ago and, as a result, the language he uses is quite different to that we use today. At first, you may find it quite difficult to understand. In Chapter 1, he uses words that are not much in use any more and phrases that were commonly used then but have less meaning now. Some examples are listed in the table below.

Word/phrase	Meaning
'emulously'	very eager to do better than someone else
'coquetry'	behaviour that is flirtatious or designed to get someone's interest or attention
'the Sawbones'	a **slang** term for a doctor
'as we were pitching it in red hot'	persuading someone in an aggressive and intense way
'the very pink of the proprieties'	someone who is very moral and law abiding

Activity 1

As you read, make a list of words and phrases that you do not know the meaning of or have fallen out of use today. Find out their meaning and create a glossary of terms for your own reference. This will make your rereading of the novella much easier and more enjoyable.

formality a scale of language use relating to the formality of the social context within which it is used. Formal or informal language can be used, depending on the context

slang distinctive words and phrases associated with informal language, often used within certain social or age groups

It is also worth noting that Stevenson's language is very **formal**. One reason for this is that the main characters are highly educated men who work in the fields of law and medicine. In Chapter 2, language is used which reflects the status of Utterson and Lanyon as educated professionals. The word 'holograph' is used to describe Jekyll's will, which means that the entire document was handwritten by Jekyll. Utterson refers to conveyancing (the legal transfer of property from one person to another) and the statute of limitations (the rules around when action can be taken in law after an event has happened). Lanyon, in conversation, makes a reference to the story of Damon and Pythias in Greek mythology, which both men understand and appreciate. This sophisticated and technical use of language is appropriate, given what the men do for a living, and it reinforces their characters.

As Victorian gentlemen, they would also take a certain pride in the formality of their speech. Their words are rarely abbreviated even in conversation. Contrast this with the informality of Poole's talk, which reflects his lower social status and limited education.

Language devices

Writers think very carefully about the language they use. This is because they want to create very deliberate effects. In your assessment, you must be able to demonstrate a clear understanding and appreciation of how Stevenson's language choices impact on the reader in *The Strange Case of Dr Jekyll and Mr Hyde*. First, you will need a very good knowledge of the most commonly used language devices or techniques used by writers. Then, you can identify, explore and analyse them.

Activity 2

1. Match each language device to the correct definition and example in the table below.

Device	Definition	Example
Simile	a comparison that says one thing *is* another	The wind whistled through the trees.
Alliteration	when something not human is said to do a human action or feel a human emotion	Pop, whizz, bang!
Metaphor	words that sound like the sound they give name to	The snake slithered slowly across the silky sand.
Personification	a comparison that uses 'like' or 'as'	The boxer was like a tiger in the ring.
Onomatopoeia	two or more words in a sentence starting with the same letter	The boxer was a tiger in the ring.

2. Scan through Chapter 1 again and identify examples of each of the language devices listed above.

Avoid feature spotting (simply identifying the language devices) in your answer because it will not secure marks on its own. You need to make it clear you understand that the writer has chosen a device deliberately, then explore and analyse the effect of it upon the reader.

Language and character

The language used to describe a character, as well as the language they use themselves, is an important way for a writer to develop the impression which that character makes on the reader. Given the frightening personality of Mr Hyde, it is not surprising that Stevenson relies heavily on the use of **figurative language** to emphasize his supernatural and evil essence. He often uses words, especially relating to animals, which remind us of Hyde's inhuman nature.

> **figurative language** the collective name for simile, metaphor and personification; language which is not to be taken literally

MR. H. B. IRVING AS MR. HYDE.
IN "DR. JEKYLL AND MR. HYDE."

276.B.   BEAGLES' POSTCARDS.

H.B. Irving's portrayal of Hyde in the 1910 stage production looks particularly villainous and animalistic

Activity 3

1. Read the passage in Chapter 10 from 'The pleasures which I made haste to seek…' to 'like a man of stone', in which Jekyll describes Hyde's nature. Then look at the table below. Notice how the student has identified the quotation and the language device or word class, but has also successfully analysed the impact of these language choices on the reader.

Quotation	Language device/word class	Analysis
'they [Hyde's actions] soon began to turn towards the monstrous'	adjective – 'monstrous'	This suggests that Hyde's behaviour is inhumane and without any sense of morality, reinforcing his animalistic, savage nature.
'a being inherently malign and villainous'	adjectives – 'malign and villainous'	This reinforces the idea that Hyde is evil and has not even the tiniest hint of goodness in him. He is portrayed as representing the very worst of man.
'drinking pleasure with bestial avidity'	metaphor	This directly relates Hyde to an animal and suggests that he greedily satisfies his evil desires, without any sense of shame or concern for anyone else.
'relentless like a man of stone'	simile	This conveys the idea that Hyde has no heart or soul and that he is an unstoppable force of evil without a conscience.

2. Read how the student has used the table above to analyse the first quotation in a PEE (Point, Evidence, Explanation) paragraph.

> Stevenson emphasizes Hyde's animal-like qualities through the use of the adjective 'monstrous' in the quotation, 'they soon began to turn towards the monstrous'. This suggests that Hyde's behaviour was inhumane and without any sense of morality, reinforcing his animalistic, savage nature.

3. Now write up three PEE paragraphs for the remaining quotations in the table, using the example above as a model.

Dialogue

The language used by a character often reveals a lot about their appearance, personality, thoughts, feelings and relationships with others. In *The Strange Case of Dr Jekyll and Mr Hyde*, it is particularly important to distinguish Hyde from Jekyll in the way that they talk as well as their actions. It is also very important to consider the **dialogue** that takes place between the characters.

> **dialogue** conversation between characters in a novel

Activity 4

1. Reread the conversation between Utterson and Jekyll in Chapter 3. Find quotations to support the following points about the personalities of each man.

   a) Jekyll is critical of Lanyon but feels the need to be diplomatic in Utterson's presence; struggling to express himself clearly; attempting desperately to persuade Utterson that he respects him and that Hyde is no longer a threat.

   b) Utterson is educated; determined to discuss the issue of Jekyll's will; keen to help his friend; unemotional, in contrast to Jekyll; diplomatic; professional.

2. Now reread Hyde's conversation with Utterson in Chapter 2 and then his conversation with Lanyon in Chapter 9. In what ways is Hyde's talk similar and in what ways does it differ in these two instances? Think about the types of sentence Hyde uses, their length and content, and the tone in which they are spoken. Why do you think this is?

Silence is another important aspect of the dialogue in the novel, with characters often failing or refusing to have certain conversations or to complete descriptions, especially of Hyde. Again, this adds to Hyde's mysterious and horrifying nature, and allows the reader to imagine what each character might say about him if they were able. (This aspect of the text is explored further on page 55.)

Language and setting

Stevenson is very successful in presenting vivid descriptions of setting, such as the block in which Jekyll lives, with its contrasting front and rear entrances as well as Hyde's Soho residence. He also reflects the personalities of the people who inhabit these places, making each building an extension of the relevant character.

The 1988 film starring Anthony Perkins recreated the sinister atmosphere of foggy, lamp-lit nights in the poor areas of Victorian London

Creating tension and suspense

Stevenson's language choices successfully create tension and suspense in the reader, a crucial feature of gothic fiction.

> **Key quotations**
>
> ... the lawyer looked at his watch. "And now, Poole, let us get to ours," he said; and taking the poker under his arm, he led the way into the yard. The scud had banked over the moon, and it was now quite dark. The wind, which only broke in puffs and draughts into that deep well of building, tossed the light of the candle to and fro about their steps, until they came into the shelter of the theatre, where they sat down silently to wait. London hummed solemnly all around; but nearer at hand; the stillness was only broken by the sound of a footfall moving to and fro along the cabinet floor. *(Chapter 8)*

Activity 5

Read the passage on the previous page, which takes place just before Utterson and Poole break down the door in Chapter 8. As you read, think about how it creates a sense of tension and suspense. Then complete the table below to analyse how Stevenson uses language to do this.

Quotation	Language device/ word class/phrase	Analysis
'looked at his watch'	phrase	
'taking the poker under his arm'		Utterson feels the need for some form of protection. This increases the sense of tension because he is not a man of action and it emphasizes just how terrified he is.
'now quite dark'		This creates an image of blackness descending on the men, reinforcing an air of uncertainty and menace, which heightens the tension.
'deep well of building'	phrase	
'The wind... tossed the light of the candle to and fro...'		
'sat down silently'		This suggests that the men were in deep thought about what they were about to do and feeling fearful and afraid.
'London hummed solemnly all around...'	personification	
'... stillness was only broken by the sound of a footfall moving to and fro along the cabinet floor.'	alliteration	

Activity 6

1. Read the passage below, thinking about how Stevenson uses language to create a sense of tension and suspense. Select about ten relevant quotations. Then create a partially completed table like the one in Activity 5 and ask your partner to complete it.

> **Key quotations**
>
> It was a wild, cold, seasonable night of March, with a pale moon, lying on her back as though the wind had tilted her, and a flying wrack of the most diaphanous and lawny texture. The wind made talking difficult, and flecked the blood into the face. It seemed to have swept the streets unusually bare of passengers, besides; for Mr Utterson thought he had never seen that part of London so deserted. He could have wished it otherwise; never in his life had he been conscious of so sharp a wish to see and touch his fellow-creatures; for struggle as he might, there was borne in upon his mind a crushing anticipation of calamity. The square, when they got there, was all full of wind and dust, and the thin trees in the garden were lashing themselves along the railing. Poole, who had kept all the way a pace or two ahead, now pulled up in the middle of the pavement, and in spite of the biting weather, took off his hat and mopped his brow with a red pocket-handkerchief. But for all the hurry of his coming, these were not the dews of exertion that he wiped away, but the moisture of some strangling anguish; for his face was white and his voice, when he spoke, harsh and broken.
> *(Chapter 8)*

2. Review the table completed by your partner and add to it if necessary. Then use it as a plan to write an extended paragraph analysing how Stevenson successfully uses language to create suspense and tension in Chapter 8.

Analysing language choices

Upgrade

Remember to identify and explore word classes, such as adjectives, verbs and adverbs, which the writer uses for effect. Use words like 'implies', 'suggests', 'reinforces' and 'conveys' to show the examiner that you are moving from identification into analysis.

Explaining language choices

An understanding of the language of *The Strange Case of Dr Jekyll and Mr Hyde* is necessary to demonstrate that the writer has deliberately chosen specific language devices, words and phrases to reinforce his ideas in relation to characters, themes and setting.

The duality of man

Duality is a key theme within the novella, closely linked to the idea of good versus evil. Jekyll's scientific work involves separating the good and evil within himself. He does this for selfish reasons, sparked by his desire to indulge his darker desires and fancies, while still maintaining his outwardly respectable image, without any sense of shame or guilt. His experiment is a failure in one sense, as he does not manage to distil two separate and wholly opposite entities of good and evil. He remains a mixture of good and evil in his normal state while managing to release his evil self as Hyde.

One debate centres on whether this evil self represents a small part of all our personalities or whether it represents the core of our being, which is kept in check and under control by the civilizing norms and influences of society. *The Strange Case of Dr Jekyll and Mr Hyde* seems to argue that once unleashed, evil is an uncontainable force which dominates and diminishes good. As Hyde grows in force and strength, Jekyll is seen to weaken.

It is the Jekyll/Hyde relationship that best explores the theme of the duality of man, but it is also explored throughout the novella in other ways; for example, in the way Utterson is portrayed at the very beginning and also in the contrasting natures of the lawyer and his distant cousin, Enfield. It is reflected in the structural split between first- and third-person narrations, and symbolically through the description of Jekyll's sprawling residence. The building's well-presented, ornate front entrance symbolizes the upright Jekyll, contrasting with the dilapidated and shabby rear entrance, which represents Hyde. These two aspects of the house interconnect, and the rooms and passages within are described as a labyrinth. The house could thus be seen as a metaphor for the complex workings of the human mind, home to both good and evil possibilities.

THE FEATURES SEEMED TO MELT AND ALTER

Edmund Sullivan's illustration in the 1928 publication shows the good and evil sides of Jekyll's character

Activity 1

Write a paragraph exploring how Stevenson links the theme of the duality of man with the description of Jekyll's residence. Try to include some of the words below in your answer.

- description
- possesses
- labyrinth
- well-presented
- good
- intricate
- rundown
- evil
- complicated
- metaphor
- duality of man
- brain

Secrecy and hypocrisy

There are many times when characters in the novella swear others to secrecy or agree not to talk about a certain topic or event ever again. After discussing Hyde's relationship with Jekyll, Utterson's cousin Enfield suggests they "never refer to this again" *(Chapter 1)*. In Chapter 3, Jekyll implores Utterson to let the same topic 'sleep' and later Lanyon refuses to share what he witnessed and later heard from Jekyll with a firm "I cannot tell you" *(Chapter 6)*. Such secrecies are important in creating the air of mystery and suspense that eventually begins to reveal itself.

Other secrets remain at the end, such as the nature of Hyde's other crimes and the detail of Jekyll's youthful and less savoury activities, as well as those of Utterson. In addition, of course, nothing is ever revealed about the science behind Jekyll's experiments.

The idea of secrecy is reinforced symbolically in the novella through the locking away of documents to be read later, the locking and unlocking of doors and the closing of windows.

The notion of secrecy in the novel is closely linked to the theme of hypocrisy. Stevenson's work is a criticism of Victorian society at the time of his writing, which was obsessed with the outward appearance of respectability and decorum. The reality, however, was very different, with seemingly respectable, middle-class gentlemen participating in sexual activities and the abuse of alcohol and drugs, which they were desperate to keep secret from family, friends and wider society. Note how desperate Utterson, a lawyer, is to protect Jekyll even when he suspects him of sheltering the murderer of Sir Danvers Carew and his hypocrisy in not sharing what he suspects with the police.

This poster for the 1920 film shows Hyde enjoying the social 'evils' of alcohol and women, presumably 'of easy virtue'

This hypocrisy relates back to the first theme of the dual nature of man. Those who meet Hyde regularly state an inability to describe and explain fully the disgust created by their encounter. Enfield, Lanyon and even Utterson all fail to articulate precisely the experience of meeting Hyde, although they all confess that they can recall his features clearly. Here, Stevenson is alluding to the inability of Victorian society to recognize the evil that lurked under the surface, at its heart. These fine, righteous and upstanding characters are portrayed as hypocrites who cannot see the evil that lies within their own natures. The disgust they feel in meeting Hyde is also a disgust with themselves for their own evil side, which they cannot even acknowledge.

Activity 2

Using the notes made for Plot and Structure Activity 6, prepare a three-minute PowerPoint presentation for the rest of your class about the themes of secrecy and hypocrisy in the novella.

Repressed desires

The theme of secrecy and hypocrisy also relates to the idea of repressed desires, particularly those of a sexual nature. The novella is full of men who are apparently single or who lack a positive, functioning and enriching relationship with women. Enfield, Lanyon, Utterson and Jekyll are all portrayed as living lives devoid of female companionship and none have married. Furthermore, there are very few women in the novella and none of any major significance. Those who do appear are not portrayed positively. The housekeeper at Hyde's Soho residence is described as having a face that is 'smoothed by hypocrisy' *(Chapter 4)* although her manners were excellent. While presented more positively as a kind-hearted and innocent figure, the maid who observes Hyde kill Sir Danvers Carew is also a passive victim. What she sees that night causes her to faint.

Some critics have suggested that Jekyll/Hyde may represent the repression of homosexual desire and behaviour in Victorian society, since the male characters appear to seek out and prefer male as opposed to female company. Homosexuality was something that Victorian society would have sought to keep secret, a fact which could support this interpretation.

The novella also shows how the repression of desire can have its own dangers, causing them to return with increased power. This is illustrated by how vicious and violent Hyde is when, having been repressed by Jekyll for two months, he returns with a vengeance to kill Sir Danvers Carew.

Activity 3

Do you think that there are no significant female characters in the novella because it would complicate and detract from the idea of the divided self, or is it to suggest the idea of repressed homosexuality? Explain your ideas.

Rational versus irrational

The supernatural

Utterson, like Lanyon, respresents the rational world in which everything can be explained. As a lawyer, Utterson uses logic to argue his points; these lines of enquiry lead him to the mistaken assumption about Hyde blackmailing Jekyll and his belief that his friend may be soon murdered for the contents of his will. The evidence, as Utterson reads it, points in these directions and the contemporary reader would have thought them quite sensible.

Hyde's supernatural qualities, however, remain beyond the reach of rational explanation. They are subtly hinted at in the early chapters. He is said to move at great speed and the effect he has on others suggests an otherworldly nature. Ironically, it is Utterson himself who unknowingly alludes to Hyde's supernatural origins when he says that Hyde's family could not be traced. His ghostly nature is also hinted at by the identification of the **'haunting sense'** *(Chapter 4)* that dominates those unfortunate enough to meet him.

Crime and justice

In a novella dealing with the struggle between scientific and supernatural, the law could have been considered a force for the rational. However, those searching for Hyde following the murder of Sir Danvers Carew face an impossible task in bringing him to justice. It is also clear that the law is portrayed as being guilty of self-interest and over-confidence. The police officer who visits Utterson after the murder is motivated most by the thought of promotion and shows arrogance in the belief that **"We have nothing to do but wait for him [Hyde] at the bank, and get out the handbills"** *(Chapter 4)*. Utterson plays a role in this too. He is not always honest in his dealings with the police. While he takes them directly to Hyde's residence, he remains quiet about his fears surrounding Jekyll's behaviour. He also assures Poole that he will **"be back before midnight, when we shall send for the police"** *(Chapter 8)*. He does not return, however, and the police are never called. It is also clear that the revelations contained in Lanyon's and Jekyll's papers render the law useless and ineffective.

Conventional versus unconventional science

This theme is linked closely to the opposing worlds of the rational and the supernatural. Science is one way to unravel the mysteries of the world we inhabit. The rational Lanyon's understanding of the world and life is based on research, evidence and logical explanations. Jekyll, however, explores the **'mystic and transcendental'** *(Chapter 10)* and is seen to push the boundaries of science. It is this that causes his friendship with Lanyon to break down. Utterson's reflections on this falling out are accurate but understated when he thinks, **"They have only differed on some point of science"** *(Chapter 2)*. The gap between the two men is, in fact, unbridgeable and, when Jekyll reveals his scientific knowledge to Lanyon after transforming from Hyde, it leaves Lanyon unable to carry on with his life. The whole basis of his world is shattered. In Chapter 9, he attempts to explain his position rationally by saying 'I saw what I saw, I heard what I heard' but ultimately can utter nothing more than 'my soul sickened at it'.

There is no doubt that Jekyll has not only pushed the boundaries of science but also those of morality and ethics. In creating Hyde, he has also usurped the role of God. This overreaching ruins him. Lanyon too is ruined by his rational beliefs and their failure to accommodate an alternative, despite the evidence presented before him. This leaves an interesting question for the reader: whose approach is the right one?

When discussing a particular theme, try to show your knowledge of the whole text, drawing your analysis from the whole novella to show how it develops.

The urban landscape

The setting of the novella is clearly Victorian London and this is established in the first chapter. There are also specific references to Hyde's Soho residence and Cavendish Square where Lanyon lives, which is referred to as 'that citadel of medicine' (Chapter 2). This area is still well-known today for its exclusive medical practices and cosmetic surgeries.

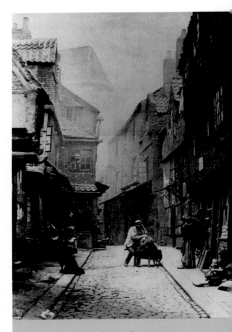

The London depicted by Stevenson is one that is well-known in modern popular culture, with its dimly-lit streets, night-time shadows, descending fog and sense of menace. If Lanyon's residence is one found in the most fashionable and sophisticated parts of contemporary London, it provides a very obvious contrast with the area where Hyde lives. His house is situated in a squalid and poverty-stricken neighbourhood beside 'a gin palace, a low French eating house, a shop for the retail of penny numbers and twopenny salads, many ragged children huddled in doorways' (Chapter 4). The squalor here reflects the equally squalid mind of Hyde – immoral and depraved. Stevenson also uses the setting of night-time Victorian London to reinforce the evil that takes place and the atmosphere of mystery and suspense that pervades the novella, for example, 'through wider labyrinths of lamplighted city...' (Chapter 2).

The slums in London at the end of the 19th century were overcrowded, rundown and disease-ridden

Friendship

Friendship is another relevant theme in the novella. Loyalty is one attribute of friendship, which ensures that Utterson pursues his quest for answers motivated by a desire to protect and help his friend Jekyll. Poole also acts out of loyalty in seeking out Utterson to come and identify the creature locked away in the room. Utterson's friendships with Lanyon and Jekyll enable him to find out the answers to the many mysteries that surround him. Less positively, it is clear that the bonds of friendship do not always facilitate honest face-to-face communication. Lanyon, for example, will not speak to Utterson about everything that he saw and heard. Note also what can happen when friendships break down, as in the case of Lanyon and Jekyll.

Activity 4

1. Another recurring theme in the novella is religion. Make a note of the references to God, Satan or the Bible. What role does the theme of religion play in the novella?

2. Identify any other themes in the novella and briefly state what role you think they play.

Writing about themes

Upgrade

Themes are important ideas that a piece of writing is concerned with. Novels and novellas usually have three or four main themes and a few others that are relevant and interesting, but less important.

When responding critically to a text, you must interpret and analyse the themes of the novella and how they are presented. You must carefully select quotations to support your views about the text.

You should also make sure you identify and analyse how the language features and the form and structure used by the writer affect how the reader responds to the themes, explaining if you find these approaches successful or not.

Skills and Practice

Exam skills

Understanding key terms and definitions

The language used when studying literature can appear difficult at first. Do not be intimidated by it though. Some of these key terms and definitions may already be familiar to you. You will need to understand all of these, as they will be used in the questions you have to answer and, of course, you will need to use them yourself in your responses.

Activity 1

1. Some key terms are listed in the table below. Match each one to its definition.

Key term	Definition
a) Insight	i) the main ideas or issues the novel is concerned with
b) Interpretation	ii) the general feeling of a passage, e.g. terrifying, suspenseful, ominous
c) Narrator	iii) another word for the story
d) Theme	iv) understanding more than just the surface meaning; reaching a deeper understanding
e) Plot	v) where the action of the text takes place
f) Tone	vi) how the writer orders the events
g) Setting	vii) the person who tells the story
h) Structure	viii) people's views and opinions about the text, often different

2. The responses opposite relate to theme, tone, setting, language and interpretations. Match each response to each key term. Some may relate to more than one.

a) Critics differ about what Hyde represents. Some argue that he is a metaphor for Jekyll's repressed sexual desires, while others feel that he is better seen as the dark, secretive side of the middle-class Victorian man who was desperate to keep his reputation.

b) The area where Hyde lives is a reflection of his evil nature. Utterson describes it using the simile, 'like a district of some city in a nightmare'. This suggests that, like a nightmare, it is a place which causes feelings of unease and fear, just as Hyde does in the people who meet him.

c) Jekyll and Lanyon are both scientists and former friends. They disagree over professional matters, as Jekyll's experiments are dismissed as 'balderdash' by Lanyon, who says that Jekyll became too 'fanciful'. It clear that Lanyon is a traditional scientist who is strongly opposed to Jekyll's more 'mystic' approach. This represents a tension between scientists at the time and their approaches to understanding the world around them.

d) A sense of mystery is established by the end of the very first chapter. The reader is already curious about what type of man Hyde is and also the exact nature of his relationship with Jekyll.

e) Stevenson moves away from the typical approaches of gothic fiction by having events take place in the city of London, which would have been instantly recognizable to many of his readers. He specifically mentions well-known locations such as Soho, which would have excited his readers.

Understanding the question

It is vital that you understand the question in your assessment. Read it at least twice and underline the key words. Make sure that you are absolutely clear about what is being asked of you before you start to plan and then write your response.

Look closely at how two students have carefully considered what their questions demand.

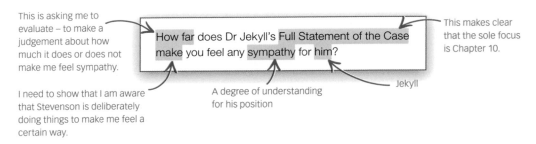

This is asking me to evaluate – to make a judgement about how much it does or does not make me feel sympathy.

How far does Dr Jekyll's Full Statement of the Case make you feel any sympathy for him?

This makes clear that the sole focus is Chapter 10.

I need to show that I am aware that Stevenson is deliberately doing things to make me feel a certain way.

A degree of understanding for his position

Jekyll

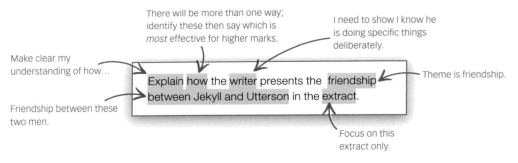

There will be more than one way; identify these then say which is *most* effective for higher marks.

I need to show I know he is doing specific things deliberately.

Make clear my understanding of how...

Explain how the writer presents the friendship between Jekyll and Utterson in the extract.

Theme is friendship.

Friendship between these two men.

Focus on this extract only.

Activity 2

Annotate the question below to show your understanding of it:

Explore the ways in which Stevenson so vividly portrays Hyde's evil.

Selecting the right question

When you have the option to choose from two questions, your first challenge is to select the right question for yourself, so that you can do your very best. This will require some careful thought and consideration, so it is not to be rushed.

If there is a printed extract in the exam paper, familiarize yourself with this first. Think about how well you know it and how confidently you could write about it. Read through the question at least twice, underlining key words and testing your understanding of the extract. Now think about what you would include in the answer. Ask yourself how many ideas you have.

Then read the alternative question. Again, do this at least twice and underline key words. Consider what you would write for your answer. Do you have more or fewer ideas for this question?

At this stage, if you are clear about which question is best for you, you can begin. If you are still unsure, it may be worth taking a few minutes to simply bullet point some ideas that you would include in answer to each question before making a decision. This whole process should take no more than ten minutes.

Extract-based questions

If you have an extract printed in the exam paper, the extract itself will have been selected because it is significant. Read the printed extract at least twice and underline the key words. Then read the extract with the question in mind. As you read, highlight, underline and make short notes in the margin, focusing your attention on those parts of the extract that you think are relevant to the question or questions. Then read the question(s) again before reading the extract once more. Again, read actively – highlighting, underlining and making notes as appropriate.

Think about:

- ✔ What has happened before and after the extract?
- ✔ Who is narrating? Is it a third- or first-person narration?
- ✔ What form does the narration take? Is it Lanyon's or Jekyll's testimony, for example?
- ✔ What does the extract reveal about the characters involved, their personalities and relationships to one another?
- ✔ What about the tone and setting of the extract?
- ✔ Is there tension or suspense?
- ✔ Consider the language used in the extract and how this relates to the theme, portrayal of character, creation of suspense or horror.
- ✔ How are sentences written to have an impact on the reader?

Close, active reading

Maximise time by being active as you closely read the extract you are asked to write about. Underline, highlight and make short notes or annotations in the margin that are relevant to the question and your response to it.

The following is an example of how one student made notes and highlighted useful words and phrases while they read through an extract from Chapter 3 for the first time.

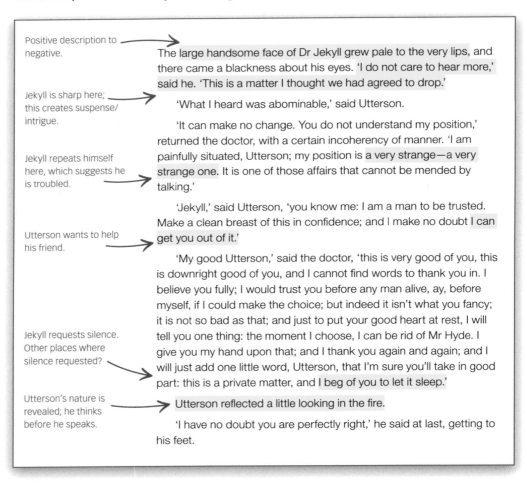

Positive description to negative.

The large handsome face of Dr Jekyll grew pale to the very lips, and there came a blackness about his eyes. 'I do not care to hear more,' said he. 'This is a matter I thought we had agreed to drop.'

Jekyll is sharp here; this creates suspense/intrigue.

'What I heard was abominable,' said Utterson.

'It can make no change. You do not understand my position,' returned the doctor, with a certain incoherency of manner. 'I am painfully situated, Utterson; my position is a very strange—a very strange one. It is one of those affairs that cannot be mended by talking.'

Jekyll repeats himself here, which suggests he is troubled.

'Jekyll,' said Utterson, 'you know me: I am a man to be trusted. Make a clean breast of this in confidence; and I make no doubt I can get you out of it.'

Utterson wants to help his friend.

'My good Utterson,' said the doctor, 'this is very good of you, this is downright good of you, and I cannot find words to thank you in. I believe you fully; I would trust you before any man alive, ay, before myself, if I could make the choice; but indeed it isn't what you fancy; it is not so bad as that; and just to put your good heart at rest, I will tell you one thing: the moment I choose, I can be rid of Mr Hyde. I give you my hand upon that; and I thank you again and again; and I will just add one little word, Utterson, that I'm sure you'll take in good part: this is a private matter, and I beg of you to let it sleep.'

Jekyll requests silence. Other places where silence requested?

Utterson reflected a little looking in the fire.

Utterson's nature is revealed; he thinks before he speaks.

'I have no doubt you are perfectly right,' he said at last, getting to his feet.

Activity 3

a) Look at the sample questions on pages 71 to 72. If the questions are based on a printed extract read the extract as well. Underline the key words in the question(s) first and then make notes to be sure you are clear about what you need to do in your response.

b) Then read the passage actively and closely, underlining, highlighting and making short notes in the margin to help you with your response. Discuss these with a partner and add to your notes if necessary.

c) Now write the response.

Writer's craft questions

If you are asked a question on the writer's craft, it may ask you to explain, for example, how the writer creates suspense, makes a particular passage frightening, or increases or reduces your sympathy for a character. This is called the writer's craft. This question requires **comment**, **criticism** and **analysis**.

Comment: requires you to discuss and explain in detail, revealing what you know about how characters are portrayed; how themes are presented and developed; and how specific outcomes are achieved.

Criticize: does not mean simply being critical or negative about the text. It requires you to write about the novella as a critic of literature and discuss in depth; it demands some form of evaluation, a judgement about what is successful and why.

Analyse: means that you must go beyond the surface to explain why characters are portrayed as they are and what function they play; why and how themes are presented as they are; and how and why the writer achieves his intended outcomes.

Follow the procedure outlined on page 62, which makes clear how you should read the question and ensure that you understand what is being asked of you. Once you have done that, you are ready to plan your response.

Planning your response

It is really important that you plan what you are going to write. You must resist the urge to start writing immediately. Better answers will have an organization and structure to them that can only come through planning.

Different people plan in different ways. Think about what works best for you, be it:

- a concept map
- a spider diagram
- a mind map
- bullet points
- a grid.

The following student has used a concept map to formulate their ideas about a Higher Tier question asking how much sympathy they feel for Jekyll.

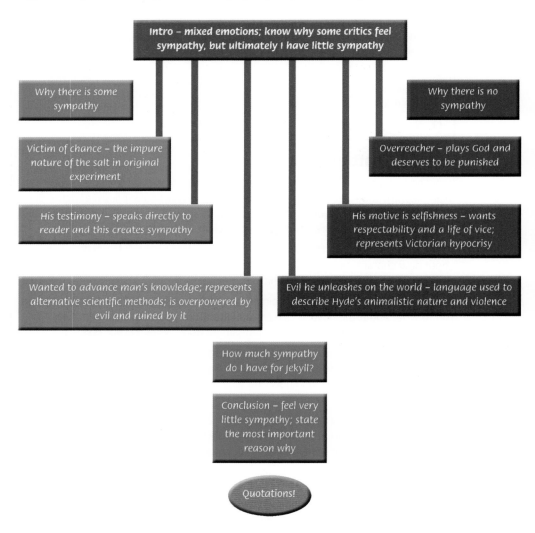

Activity 4

1. The concept map opposite is a good initial plan. Complete the table to explain why.

Focus	Evidence
There is a balanced argument.	The student reveals reasons why some think there is sympathy even though they do not feel it. This shows a good understanding of the text.
Despite the balance, the student's viewpoint is clear and stated at the beginning.	
The essay has a sense of structure.	
The student is aware of different interpretations.	
The student knows to include analysis of language features.	
There is appreciation that the character is a creation.	
The student appreciates the writer's craft.	
There is awareness of the importance of quotations.	
There is evidence of evaluation.	

2. Now use the plan above to write a response to the question: 'How much sympathy do you feel for Jekyll?'

Writing your answer

Spelling, punctuation and grammar

You need to pay close attention to the quality of your written communication, which includes your spelling, punctuation and grammar. You should ensure that your text is legible and that spelling, punctuation and grammar are accurate so that meaning is clear.

This means you must present your handwriting in a way that is easy for the examiner to read. You must also use capital letters, full stops, commas and other relevant forms of punctuation correctly. It is also important to write using accurate grammar, avoiding slang. All of the above will ensure that what you want to say is conveyed clearly and appropriately.

You will have done several practice essays before you sit your exam. In the exam, make sure that you read the question(s) carefully and answer exactly what is being asked of you. Avoid the temptation to rewrite what you wrote in practice essays, if it is not relevant.

Working with quotations

It is vital that you support your ideas with relevant quotations. These can be a sentence, phrase or even just a word from the novella, as long as they are carefully chosen. Doing this strengthens the points you are make. By exploring, analysing and evaluating these quotations, you can achieve higher marks. The starting point, however, is making sure that the quotations you select are the most relevant to the points you wish to make.

Activity 5

1. The following quotations relate to the themes of secrecy, the duality of man and the idea of rational thought versus the supernatural. Copy the table opposite and put each quotation into the correct column.

    ❝a hide-bound pedant❞

    ❝losing hold of my original and better self❞

    ❝Let us make a bargain never to refer to this again❞

    ❝balderdash❞

    ❝must have secrets of his own: black secrets❞

    ❝cold… yet somehow lovable❞

    ❝the windows are always shut❞

    ❝a profound duplicity of life❞

    ❝that man is not truly one, but truly two❞

    ❝the cancer of some concealed disgrace❞

    ❝It is more than ten years since Henry Jekyll became too fanciful❞

    ❝I beg of you to let this sleep❞

    ❝a lover of the sane and customary sides of life, to whom the fanciful was the immodest❞

Secrecy	The duality of man	Rational thought versus the supernatural

2. Find appropriate quotations from Chapters 1–4 to support the following themes:

- blackmail
- London at night
- females being portrayed negatively.

Analysing and evaluating supporting quotations

Many of the previous activities in this book will have helped you to develop the skills of analysing and evaluating quotations so that you can gain higher marks.

You must show that you understand and appreciate that Stevenson chooses his words carefully and deliberately to create very specific effects. This skill is not easy and takes practice. For example, Stevenson describes Hyde as 'ape-like'. He is not saying Hyde looks exactly like an ape or that he walks on all fours. Instead, he is saying that Hyde has the qualities of an ape – he is dangerous, wild and untamed, unpredictable, capable of incredible power and strength, savage.

Look at the response below in which a student demonstrates the ability to analyse the quotation he has selected to support his idea. It also evaluates, which means that it makes a judgement about whether or not the language used by the writer is successful in conveying his ideas.

Student knows language devices.

Point is clearly expressed.

Stevenson describes Hyde using language which clearly emphasizes an animalistic nature. He uses the alliteration, 'snarled aloud into a savage laugh' to successfully reinforce his vicious and wild temperament. The verb 'snarled' conjures images of terrifying bared teeth that have the potential to rip and tear at flesh.

Supporting quotation is well-chosen, accurate.

Makes analytical comment.

Student knows word classes.

Activity 6

Analyse and evaluate the following quotations from the novella. Use the model on page 69 to help you. Try to identify the language device and/or word class; use words like 'emphasizes', 'suggests', 'reinforces' and 'implies'.

a) 'an aged and beautiful gentleman with white hair'

b) 'I put him back, conscious at his touch of a certain icy pang along my blood'

c) 'the low growl of London from all around'

What not to do in an exam answer

What follows is a checklist of things you should avoid when preparing for and writing your examination response.

✗ Do not simply rewrite a practice essay which you got a good mark for – especially if it doesn't specifically answer your exam question!

✗ Do not write a response which has not been planned.

✗ Do not write a long-winded introduction that says what you will write about.

✗ Do not write about areas of the novella other than the extract if you are told not to.

✗ Do not include large chunks of supporting quotations that are several sentences long.

✗ Do not simply identify use of simile, metaphor, or personification, for example, if it is not relevant, and do not forget to comment on or analyse their impact.

✗ Do not write about the life of the author or the time at which the novel was written unless directly relevant to your answer.

Remember to comment on and analyse the impact of the supporting quotations which you include in your response.

It is vital to leave yourself enough time to complete your response. If you run out of time and have lots you would still like to include, you could, as a last resort, quickly bullet-point these ideas.

Sample questions

1

Foundation Tier

Look at the extract at the beginning of Chapter 4 from 'Although a fog rolled over the city...' to '... the maid fainted.'

a) Outline the key events that **lead up to** this extract.

b) Explain how the writer presents terror in this extract.

Use **evidence** from the extract to support your answer.

c) From this extract, what do you learn about the character of Hyde?

Use **evidence** from the extract to support your answer.

d) In this extract we see the actions of Mr Hyde. Explain how Mr Hyde is described in **one other** part of the novel.

Use examples of the writer's language to support your answer.

2

Higher Tier

Look at the extract at the beginning of Chapter 4 from 'Although a fog rolled over the city...' to '... the maid fainted.'

a) From the extract, what do you discover about the character of Hyde?

Use **evidence** from the extract to support your answer.

b) Comment on the effect of the language used to present Hyde in the extract.

Use examples of the writer's language from the extract.

c) Explore the significance of violence and crime in this extract.

Use **evidence** from the extract to support your answer.

d) Explore the significance of violence and crime in **one other** part of the novel.

Use examples of the writer's language to support your answer.

3

Foundation Tier

Look at the extract from Chapter 2 from 'From that time forward, Mr Utterson began to haunt the door...' to '... "Mr Hyde, I think?"'

Either a)

What do you find tense about the build up to Hyde and Utterson's meeting in this extract?

You should consider:

- the thoughts of Mr Utterson before the scene
- the setting
- the language Stevenson uses.

Or b)

Explore **one** or **two** moments in the novel when you think friendship is particularly important.

Remember to support your ideas with details from the novel.

4

Higher Tier

Look at the extract from Chapter 2 from 'From that time forward, Mr Utterson began to haunt the door...' to '... "Mr Hyde, I think?"'

Either a)

How does Stevenson build up tension in this extract?

Or b)

How does Stevenson make friendship important in the novel?

Remember to support your ideas with details from the novel.

Sample answers

Sample answer 1

Look closely at the following response. It explores the language used to describe Hyde when he tramples over the young girl in Chapter 1.

Stevenson employs pathetic fallacy to hint at the evil to come when he describes the time and place where the action occurs as 'some place at the end of the world, about three o'clock of a black winter morning'. The metaphor 'black' creates an ominous tone and a sense of suspense in the reader about what is to follow. Hyde is initially described as 'stumping along.' This emotive verb suggests a forcefulness about Hyde, even in the manner of his walking, and subtly suggests that violence lurks close to the surface of this individual. The power of Hyde's action as he 'trampled' over the young victim is reinforced through another emotive verb. The evil of the deed lies in the adverb Stevenson uses to describe his actions, 'calmly'. This conveys Hyde's complete lack of conscience or concern for the child and reveals his totally immoral nature. The metaphor 'hellish' is used to emphasize the horrific nature of the action and it also successfully connects Hyde and the devil in the mind of the reader. A simple but powerful simile, 'like some damned Juggernaut' reinforces the power of Hyde and emphasizes his truly evil nature, contrasting him with the defenceless and powerless child he steamrollers over and leaves 'screaming on the ground'.

Shows awareness of the writer's techniques.

Shows good understanding of language devices.

Shows the impact of the writer's language choices on the reader.

Shows understanding of Hyde's character.

The quotation is successfully embedded.

Evaluation is simply but clearly worded.

Sample answer 2

Look closely at the following response. It explores the portrayal of Utterson in Chapter 7.

Utterson is portrayed as enjoying one of his weekly walks with his cousin Enfield. This projects the traditional image of a respectable Victorian gentleman at his innocent leisure. His concern for his friend is evident, 'I am uneasy about poor Jekyll' and this prompts his decision to step into Jekyll's courtyard to seek him out. Utterson urges Jekyll to get out and walk in order to whip 'up the circulation'. This appears somewhat pathetic given Jekyll's current predicament and reinforces the limited insight and understanding that the lawyer has of what is happening. Jekyll's sudden and dramatic change of expression provokes an intense reaction in both Utterson and Enfield. The omniscient narration says it 'froze the very blood.' This metaphor suggests just how profound an impact even the merest glimpse of Hyde can have on the viewer as blood is the life source and Hyde is seen to be a threat to that. A contemporary reader would be full of suspense at this stage.

Shows sound understanding of the character.

Gives relevant evidence to support ideas.

Makes comment on Utterson's limited narration.

Gives relevant evidence to support ideas.

Language is well analysed.

Despite seeing this strange and curious look on Jekyll's face for only an instant, Utterson, like Enfield, is reduced to silence and they turn pale, 'with an answering horror in their eyes'. It is clear that unknown to them, they have witnessed Jekyll about to transform into Hyde – they have seen something supernatural and beyond the realm of their understanding and experience. The inability to speak of it is open to interpretation and could suggest, if Hyde is a metaphor of Victorian hypocrisy, that they have witnessed a reflection of their own evil actions. Their inability to speak is their refusal to accept their own capacity for evil.

I, however, think that their silence is because Hyde represents a pure, unadulterated form of evil and Utterson's rational mind has not got the capacity to comprehend it. When Utterson finally speaks it is to say, 'God forgive us'. Here, the lawyer is seen to seek refuge in religion and God, which reinforces the notion of good versus evil in this novella.

Structure is well analysed.

Stevenson has made the deliberate decision to keep this chapter very short. This emphasizes the speed with which the action takes place and heightens the tension as a result. It works very effectively.

Sample answer 3

Below you will find extracts from a response to the following questions:

Foundation Tier

*Look at the extract from Chapter 3 from 'The large handsome face of Dr Jekyll…'
to ' "… a very great interest in that young man" '.*

Answer both of the following questions.

a) How is the friendship between Jekyll and Utterson presented in this extract?
You should consider:

- the situation Jekyll is in
- what Jekyll and Utterson say
- the words and phrases Stevenson uses.

b) Explore any **one** or **two** moments in the novel when you think friendship is
particularly important.

Remember to support your ideas with details from the novel.

Immediately focuses on the question, with accurate comment.

Shows understanding of text linked to theme of friendship.

Shows appreciation of how Utterson is willing to help Jekyll.

Gives well-selected and accurate supporting quotations.

Gives personal opinion of Jekyll's motivation, with reasoning.

Shows appreciation of how language use and sentence structure reveal character.

a) Stevenson presents a complicated friendship. The two men are close friends and admire each other, but Jekyll will not share his secret. The conversation takes place when everyone else at the party has gone, which suggests the men's closeness. Utterson is presented as being prepared to do anything to help Jekyll, telling him that if he is in trouble he can get him out of it. This suggests he would use his skills as a lawyer to save Jekyll from any danger. They are frank in conversation which is a sign of friendship too. Jekyll tells Utterson that he does not 'care to hear more' while Utterson states bluntly 'Well, I tell you so again'.

Jekyll thanks Utterson more than once to emphasize his gratitude. He becomes incredibly complimentary, telling Utterson that he believes 'in him fully' and trusts him 'before any man alive'. I am suspicious here of Jekyll's motives, however, and suspect he is trying to cover up his lies. He repeats himself, 'a very strange — a very strange one'. This repetition suggests he is uncomfortable and thinking carefully about what he is saying.

Nevertheless, Utterson believes Jekyll when he tells him he can get rid of Hyde, 'I have no doubt you are perfectly right' and puts the friendship first, not wanting to fall out.

b) Stevenson places Utterson at the heart of the numerous friendships in the novella. This is deliberate on his part and aids the plot and structure. As Utterson moves from friend to friend in conversation, the story moves forward.

Shows clear understanding of writer's intention and structure.

In the very first pages, the theme of friendship is emphasized. Although 'cold' and 'embarrassed in discourse', Utterson is 'at friendly meetings' described as 'eminently human'. This suggests that he is most comfortable among friends and this is helped 'when the wine was to his taste', which suggests that alcohol brings him out of his shell. His friendships are based on 'blood' or the length of acquaintance. This implies a strong desire to base his friendships on much more than similar interests or shared personality traits. As a result the bonds are much stronger. Stevenson uses the simile 'like ivy' to effectively reinforce how strong and loyal a friend he is. Ivy grows quickly and clings forcibly to walls. It is not easy to remove and this suggests his loyalty and trust are long lasting.

Skilful use of embedded, supporting quotations.

Gives useful comment on the nature of Utterson's friendships.

Accurately identifies language feature and comments on it.

Stevenson emphasizes that Utterson is not one to judge his friends, stating he 'had an approved tolerance for others' and is 'inclined to help rather than to reprove'. This is stressed at the very outset of the novella so that the reader can understand and more easily accept Utterson's actions later when he suspects Jekyll has forged Hyde's signature but does not turn him in to the police. What might be seen as weakness and dishonesty is offered as loyalty and the desire to help a friend. Stevenson reinforces this idea when Utterson admits, 'I let my brother go to the devil in his own way.' The use of the word 'brother' conveys just how loyal Utterson is and the admission further reflects how tolerant he is of those he calls friend.

Gives well-selected embedded supporting quotations.

Shows awareness of writer's intention and structure.

Gives further language analysis.

Sample answer 4

Below you will find a sample response to the following question:

Higher Tier

Look at the extract from Chapter 9 from '"And now," said he, "to settle what remains..."' to '... there stood Henry Jekyll!'

Comment on the effect of the language used to create suspense in this extract.

Use examples of the writer's language from the extract.

Immediately focuses on the question; also identifies context.

This passage is full of suspense, as it is the moment when Hyde transforms back into Jekyll and effectively ruins Lanyon, the narrator here. Tension and suspense are created because Lanyon does not know the identity of the man in his room, although the reader does. I think Stevenson's language and use of punctuation when describing this change are the most successful features in creating suspense.

Gives evaluation of techniques.

Shows good understanding of the text.

Hyde's offer 'to settle what remains' creates tension instantly, as the reader is not aware of whether or not Lanyon will accept. It is also clear that the offer is intended to prove Lanyon wrong and punish his contempt for Jekyll's 'too fanciful' scientific experiments. The suspense is built upon further through the clear warning issued by Hyde, which advises Lanyon to 'think before' he answers. Hyde offers 'a new province of knowledge and new avenues to fame and power' on the one hand but also 'a prodigy to stagger the unbelief of Satan' on the other. This reminds me of the temptation of Eve by the serpent and also reinforces Hyde's evil nature. This offer, like Hyde's initial choice of Lanyon to obtain the contents of the drawer, is now seen as a deliberate ploy to get revenge on Jekyll's former friend, reinforcing Hyde's destructive nature.

Addresses the theme of Hyde's evil, supported by relevant biblical comparison.

This comment develops and supports the previous one.

Lanyon's positive response is his downfall. Suspense is created in his attempts to appear calm and collected. He pretends 'a coolness', although underneath he is very nervous and anxious. Hyde's tone is one of glee at this and he uses the rhetorical rule of three, repeating 'you' to openly mock Lanyon, who 'derided the virtue of transcendental medicine'. Further tension is created when Hyde applies the Hippocratic Oath to ensure Lanyon's silence about what follows.

Shows good understanding of the text, appreciation of language devices and awareness of tone.

Shows knowledge beyond the text.

The moment of transformation is when the suspense is at its highest. Here, Stevenson conveys the action skilfully in one paragraph composed of one short sentence followed by one long sentence and drawn out through the use of commas and hyphens. The first sentence conveys the quick action with which Hyde swallowed the potion. The second reveals a series of violent actions by the drinker, 'A cry followed; he reeled, staggered, clutched at the table and held on…'. This suggests that Hyde falls instantly under the influence of the drug and loses control of his body. His crashing around the room creates tension, as does the image of his 'injected eyes' and 'gasping with open mouth'. Lanyon is confronted by sights and sounds that frighten and terrify. Stevenson skilfully gets around the mystery of the transformation by having Hyde's features 'melt and alter'. The impact on Lanyon creates suspense because he shrinks back 'submerged in terror' against the wall, seeking refuge and protecting himself from the 'prodigy' before him. Interestingly, he uses the same word here as Hyde used before, which implies that he is now suddenly more in tune with the man he previously mocked and ridiculed.

Shows perceptive appreciation of structure.

Gives a simple but very effective comment.

Gives a very perceptive comment.

Lanyon's scream, 'O God', which he repeats twice, creates suspense because it is a desperate cry for help. With his rational world turned upside down, the scientist reverts to Christianity and God for protection. More tension is created in the revelation that incredibly Hyde has become Jekyll and through the use of punctuation. Stevenson extends the sentence with commas and hyphens again: 'pale and shaken, and half fainting, and groping before him with his hands, like a man restored from death — there stood Henry Jekyll!' He deliberately leaves the identity of Jekyll until the very end. The simile 'like a man restored from death' is a simple but powerful way to also heighten suspense because it conveys the seemingly impossible, which Lanyon has just witnessed, and draws on a terror that would have quickened the blood of the Victorian reader – the dead coming back to life. This simile is also powerful because it echoes Lanyon's earlier statement in Chapter 6 that Jekyll was 'dead' to him.

Gives perceptive comment.

Shows perceptive awareness of writer's craft and sentence structure.

Evaluates the writer's language choices.

Analyses language and good understanding of the novella.

In conclusion, Stevenson very successfully creates tension here through his skill as a writer. He uses punctuation and language to reinforce this sense of suspense in his reader.

Analyses and evaluates to the end.

Glossary

alliteration repetition of the same letter or sound at the beginning of words close to each other

alter ego an alternative personality

animalistic resembling an animal

chronological order the presentation of events in a story in the order in which they actually occurred

confessional form a type of writing in which the characters reveal their innermost thoughts, motivations and actions, so mysteries or secrets are finally revealed

dialogue conversation between characters in a novel

duality the quality of being two things or split into two parts; the idea that we have two sides to our natures

figurative language the collective name for simile, metaphor and personification; language which is not to be taken literally

first-person narration a story told from the narrator's point of view, using the pronouns 'I' or 'me'

formality a scale of language use relating to the formality of the social context within which it is used. Formal or informal language can be used, depending on the context

gothic fiction a literary style characterized by tales of horror and the supernatural

irony the discrepancy between what a character could be expected to do and what they actually do, often for comic effect

labyrinthine complex; maze-like

linear narrative the presentation of events in a story in the order in which they actually occurred

metaphor a comparison of one thing to another to make a description more vivid; a metaphor states that one thing *is* the other

multiple perspective narration a story told from the point of view of more than one narrator

narrator the person who tells a story

nocturnal relating to the night

non-linear narrative the presentation of events in a story in a different order to that in which they occurred

novella a prose text which is longer than a short story but shorter than a standard novel

onomatopoeia the use of words which sound like the thing or process they describe

overreacher someone who pushes the boundaries of science in their quest for knowledge and is ruined as a result

personification a type of metaphor where human qualities are given to objects or ideas

simile a comparison of one thing to another to make a description more vivid, using the words 'like' or 'as' to make the comparison

slang distinctive words and phrases associated with informal language, often used within certain social or age groups

sub-genre a smaller grouping within a literary genre

symbolism using something to represent a concept, idea or theme in a novel

testimony a sub-genre of gothic fiction in which a story is told through personal documents like letters or confessions

third-person narration a story told from the perspective of a character or voice outside the story, using the pronouns 'he' and 'she'; this perspective could be limited or it could be 'omniscient' – aware of the thoughts and feelings of all the characters

UNIVERSITY PRESS

Great Clarendon Street, Oxford OX2 6DP

Oxford University Press is a department of the University of Oxford.
It furthers the University's objective of excellence in research,
scholarship, and education by publishing worldwide in

Oxford   New York

Auckland   Cape Town   Dar es Salaam   Hong Kong   Karachi
Kuala Lumpur   Madrid   Melbourne   Mexico City   Nairobi
New Delhi   Shanghai   Taipei   Toronto

With offices in

Argentina   Austria   Brazil   Chile   Czech Republic   France   Greece
Guatemala   Hungary   Italy   Japan   Poland   Portugal   Singapore
South Korea   Switzerland   Thailand   Turkey   Ukraine   Vietnam

Oxford is a registered trade mark of Oxford University Press
in the UK and in certain other countries

British Library Cataloguing in Publication Data

Data available

ISBN 978-0-19-912878-5

10 9 8 7 6 5 4 3 2 1

MIX
Paper from
responsible sources
FSC® C007785

Printed in Great Britain by Bell and Bain Ltd., Glasgow

Acknowledgements

Cover: Getty Images

p6: World History Archive/Alamy; **p10:** Mary Evans Picture Library/
Alamy; **p16:** AF archive/Alamy; **p18:** World History Archive/Alamy;
p22: 2d Alan King/Alamy; **p24 & p25:** ©Heritage Images/Corbis;
p27: The Print Collector/Alamy; **p28:** Pictorial Press Ltd/Alamy;
p30: Photos 12/Alamy; **p33:** Photos 12/Alamy; **p34:** World History
Archive/Alamy; **p35:** AF archive/Alamy; **p36:** © Underwood &
Underwood/Corbis; **p48:** Mary Evans Picture Library/Alamy;
p51: Photos 12/Alamy; **p54:** World History Archive/Alamy;
p55: Photos 12/Alamy; **p58:** The Art Archive/Alamy.